WHEN LOVE
AND MONEY
ARE GONE

WHEN LOVE AND MONEY ARE GONE

True stories of women
and financial independence

ELSA LIM

PARTRIDGE

To order additional copies of this book, contact
Toll Free 800 101 2657 (Singapore)
Toll Free 1 800 81 7340 (Malaysia)
orders.singapore@partridgepublishing.com

www.partridgepublishing.com/singapore

CONTENTS

Foreword... vii

Why I wrote this book ix

PART 1: Rude Awakening 1

The Other Woman 3

The Trailing Spouse 10

Married to A Mama's Boy 16

PART 2: Breaking Through 23

I am the Captain of my soul....................... 25

Minister of Home Affairs........................... 31

The Power of Giving 39

PART 3: Growing and Becoming 45

Learning Never Stops................................. 47

Taming the Debt Monster.......................... 53

Success is the Best Medicine....................... 61

The Accidental Entrepreneur...................... 71

PART 4: Leaning In with Tara Kimbrell Cole .. 81

An Interview 83

PART 5: Next Steps..93

Let's Improve our Financial Fitness 95

The Dangers of 'Money Fog' 98

A Word about Financial Freedom................................ 100

Money Fitness Coaching... 102

Finally 104

Where to Find Help and Information 105

FOREWORD

L ike most Asian women, I grew up in a patriarchal culture, believing that a man must take care of the money while the woman's duty is to take care of the children and keep the home clean and comfortable.

If my mother had strictly followed this 'feminine' role that culture prescribed, she and her 11 young children would have suffered when my father's business went under just before he died. If she had not stashed away some assets in the form of jewellery and saved money for a rainy day; my siblings and I would surely not have a good start in life.

My mother-in-law was another woman who defied the cultural norm. As a homemaker who had no regular income of her own and very little education, she bought blue chip stocks, opened fixed deposit bank accounts, traded in the stock market and bought a landed property - again by practising good financial habits.

These are forward thinking women I admired and learned from. Their foresight in managing their finances and building a nest egg for their families without any formal financial education is highly commendable.

That's why I heartily endorse and congratulate Elsa for writing this engaging and thought provoking book – full of cautionary examples as well as inspirational stories of women taking decisive action to control their financial destinies.

I know Elsa well, having worked with her as my company's financial adviser from 2009 - 2015. Elsa is also the Honorary Secretary of IWFCI (International Women's Federation of Commerce and Industry) Singapore. She is passionate about helping women to reach their full potential as individuals, to build better lives for themselves and their families – with or without their men!

Her empathy allows her to step into the shoes of the women she interviews, telling their stories from their unique perspectives. Rather than writing yet another book on personal finance with facts and figures, she has chosen to highlight strong role models like Veronica Tan and Tara Kimbrell Cole – women whom I know and greatly admire for their outstanding achievements. We can all learn from these women and their real life experiences breaking free of the constraints and obstacles that hold them back from financial independence.

Today, women are no longer confined to the kitchen – cooking, waiting for our husband to come back and serving him. We have as much opportunity as men in all areas, from education to business. Women are also holding key positions in organisations and governments. In whatever role we find ourselves, we need to be wise about our own money and plan our financial safety nets for the worse case scenarios – just like what my mother and mother-in-law did.

I believe financial independence does not mean the blind pursuit of wealth at any cost. It is about careful planning and the avoidance of uncontrolled debt and financial loss, so that we can continue to live with dignity, abundance and fulfillment – without depending on handouts and losing our souls.

Mrs Ann Phua
President,
International Women's Federation of Commerce and Industry (Singapore)

WHY I WROTE THIS BOOK

I grew up not fully understanding what money is, how it can be used and abused, and its seductive power to bring people together or break relationships apart.

Like all well-brought-up Chinese girls from respectable Chinese families, I grew up in an environment where money was never discussed in everyday conversation. In the first place, there was never a need to discuss it or worry about it because as a child, I had a very comfortable life. Whatever I wanted, my dear Daddy was my ATM, always ready to pull out his wallet and flash his Diners or American Express.

We never suffered any lack or went hungry. Every day for many years, I was given a few dollars to spend for lunch at the school canteen and that was that. I never felt the need to save or work for something that I really wanted. I did not have to worry about bills. I never saw any bills – they were simply other people's problem, not mine.

In the 1960s and 1970s when I was growing up, first in Kuala Lumpur and then in Singapore, life revolved around going to school, tuition (which I hated), and swimming and ballet lessons (which I loved). By the standards of those days, my two younger brothers and I were privileged kids. My single Dad was a sought-after architect who ran his own practice and appreciated the finer things in life. Our weekends were spent socialising with his many well-to-do friends, dining in restaurants or hanging out at the country club. We often went to the park or cycled around our quiet suburban neighbourhood.

During school holidays, we'd pile into Dad's silver Holden (considered a status symbol then) and drive up country to Penang, Fraser's Hill or Cameron Highlands.

I always look back at my childhood with a touch of nostalgia and a tinge of regret because it is so very different from my life today. It seemed as if I had lived in Peter Pan's "Neverland," where life was idyllic and money grew on trees. Put it bluntly, I was a financial infant.

I believe that we were all financial infants at some point in our lives. For most people, financial infancy ends with a significant life event such as marriage, buying a home, parenthood, and starting a career or business. For me, it ended when my beloved Daddy lost his business, suffered a stroke and then a second stroke, which killed him at the age of 49. This event changed my life, as I recount in the opening story of this book, *The Other Woman*.

I wrote this book because I realised that not everyone grows out of financial infanthood. Some of us are like foetuses still attached to the idea that even if we don't do anything to manage our finances, someone – our employers or the government – will continue to feed us. Life will still continue as per normal, as long as somebody picks up our bills and gives us a job.

This was my mindset for a very long time. My father's death did not immediately turn me into a financially responsible woman overnight. In my 20s, I was still happily enjoying the money I earned, spending it on luxuries like designer clothes and handbags, and hanging out with my friends at the latest nightspots and the hippest restaurants. The 1980s was in full swing and I worked in the "cool" business of advertising and public relations, where looking good was everything.

I had zero knowledge of investments and was only dimly aware of the stock market. My only positive action with regards to money was to start three savings plans – rather reluctantly – because my insurance agent at that time assured me that the savings would come in handy when I reached my 40s and 50s.

Forties? Fifties? It was inconceivable! Like many young women, I simply didn't want to think that far. Today, I'm rather embarrassed to admit that I bought into that whole fantasy of meeting "The One" (aka Prince Charming) and settling down to a charmed life. Several of my friends achieved this goal – marrying very well to men who adored them and who were rich enough to support them in style and spoil them lavishly with vacations and bling.

But to my disappointment, it didn't happen to me! Girls who lose their beloved fathers early often search for Daddy in their relationships and I was no exception. After several failed relationships, I realised that I had to conquer my own demons, deal with my own baggage and learn to be happy on my own – whether Prince Charming shows up or not!

In my 40s, I made several sharp hairpin turns in my long and winding journey to discover myself. I became a financial adviser and a Christian. I also studied psychotherapy. I stopped focusing on fantasy and started facing reality. I stopped being self-absorbed and started becoming more aware of how little time I have to make a difference in the lives of others. It was a complete mental, emotional, spiritual and financial revolution in the way I responded to the world. I finally understood money. As a financial adviser, I had to be financially literate myself.

In my 14 years as a financial adviser, I've met many women who still haven't come to grips with managing their money and financial health. They still carried the baggage that I used to carry – the fantasy that Prince Charming will take care of everything.

The most frequent excuses I hear? "My husband handles everything," or "I don't know what my husband has done with our money, ask him." I've also met smart, capable women who were forced to sacrifice their careers and financial independence in order to care for their loved ones.

They may be savvy with money, but their lack of a stable income and ability to save for retirement puts them at a disadvantage.

By nature, we women have always tended to put the needs of our loved ones before our own. We are resigned to the fact that we will always earn less because we interrupt our careers to care for our families. Therefore, why should we fight for more?

Despite the fact that more and more women are graduating with degrees, entering the workforce and climbing the corporate ladder, survey after survey all over the world have shown that women are not only paid less than men, they are often worse off financially than men in a divorce, and have less retirement savings.

However, at the other end of the spectrum, I see an encouraging trend. Leading this trend are women who are aware of the need to take charge of their financial futures and are doing something about it – whether starting their own businesses or managing their money wisely so that they can live the life they love, having more than enough.

I did not set out to write a purely financial advice book. There are too many books that claim to lead you to the "Promised Land" of wealth and dreams coming true if you follow their advice. There are many financial advisers who will crunch numbers and statistics advising you on what and how to invest.

But know this: Financial health is more than just having a fat bank account, nice clothes and a beautiful home; it is about dealing with the issues that hold you back from living a fulfilling life.

Not having enough money is a sign that we are not managing our financial health. We don't have financial health because we don't know who we are and what we want. We spend money mindlessly buying lots of bright, shiny objects that we later get bored with and throw away.

We tend to direct our energy (and money) towards the easy decisions like "Where shall I go for my vacation?" rather than the big questions of "How can I live a truly meaningful life and manage myself and my money to achieve my goals?"

That's why women need to talk about this. This book contains stories based on conversations that I've had with 10 women over the course of six months.

They were quite reluctant at first to bare their hearts and secrets, but they relented after they learnt that their experiences may be helpful to other women facing similar circumstances such as the death of a spouse and child or dealing with cancer and divorce.

All the stories are real, but in order to respect their privacy, none of the women's real names and personal details have been revealed (with the exception of Lisa Ng, Veronica Tan and Tara Kimbrell Cole). Every story ends with a reflection on the financial lessons learnt.

I have organised the stories in four main parts. In Part One, which I call *Rude Awakening*, I recount stories of shock, despair and desperation when one is hit by a major personal and financial crisis.

The opening story, *The Other Woman*, is in fact my own memoir of that fateful day when I learnt of the financial mess my father left behind when he died, and the aftershocks that followed.

In Part Two of the book entitled *Breaking Through*, I tell the stories of three brave women who survived their personal and financial tsunamis to emerge stronger and wiser – with new goals, passion and purpose.

In Part Three, *Growing and Becoming*, I profile two women who are thriving in different stages of life, namely retirement and mid-career, and how they have developed the mindset that kept them financially healthy. As more and more women become entrepreneurs, I'm also thrilled that two of my friends, Lisa Ng and Veronica Tan, agreed to share their personal stories and struggles with me in this section.

In Part Four, my interview with business coach Tara Kimbrell Cole presents an overview of how women can break free from the constraints that hold them back from leading truly fulfilling and financially independent lives.

My final chapter outlines some practical ideas on how you can benefit from taking care of your financial health.

I hope that all the stories in this book will resonate with you and provide inspiration and encouragement in your life journey. Whatever financial struggles or relationship problems you may be going through, I want you to know that you are stronger than you think! Women have broken through, and will keep on breaking through. And so will you.

Elsa Lim
Money Fit Coach
elsa@moneyfitcoach.com
www.moneyfitcoach.com

PART 1:

Rude Awakening

THE OTHER WOMAN

At the age 20, my comfortable world came crashing down. It was the greatest financial life lesson I had to learn and so, I would like to begin this book by sharing with you my own personal story ...

"I want $15,000! I've spent all my savings on your father; it's only fair that your family pays me back!" It wasn't a friendly request. The woman stared at us, her large eyes piercing through us like daggers.

I couldn't believe what I heard. Could this really be Angie, Dad's live-in partner for the last three years? The woman who used to smile and greet us warmly? The woman whom we saw as a member of the family? Why has she suddenly become so hostile towards us, barely 48 hours after my father died of a heart attack?

My 20-year-old brain just couldn't (or wouldn't) process the information. I was numb with worry and fear, as were my younger brothers – mere lads who only three days before, were playing soccer and building model airplanes.

We had received the shocking news of Dad's sudden death at the worst possible time – on the first evening of our vacation on the beautiful island of Tioman in Malaysia. My brothers, cousins and I had been planning our very first independent vacation (with no adults) for ages. We had hired a car and driven to Mersing on the east coast of Johore and boarded a fishing boat to Tioman. The entire trip took a day's journey in the 1970s. It was dark when we reached the island and we were enjoying our barbeque dinner when we were told of the tragedy.

Dad apparently felt unwell and went to the doctor on the afternoon of February 16, 1979. When he reached the clinic, he collapsed and died on the way to the hospital. The three of us had just spent Chinese New Year together with Dad a week before. He had driven from Kuala Lumpur, where he lived with Angie, to Singapore, where the three of us went to school.

Dad's architecture practice had a great start in the 1960s, when the newly independent Federation of Malaya and Singapore saw a great deal of building and construction activity. Fresh from Harvard's School of Design, Dad not only worked hard but also played hard. He was a bon vivant and knew all the movers and shakers in KL who awarded him lucrative contracts all over Malaysia.

My parents broke up when I was nine. They had different temperaments, which made the marriage highly combustible. It was the swinging 60s. My mother was happy to let Dad have custody of the kids and took off for Europe to chase her own dreams. She was tired of being a housewife and wanted to study languages and become an interpreter. Plagued by depression, she overdosed on sleeping pills and died in her early 40s. My brothers and I grew up under the care of our paternal grandma and our loving, jolly, larger-than-life Daddy.

As I shared in the opening chapter of this book, I was fresh out of school, a spoilt and sheltered brat whose only interests in life was pop music and fashion. We had no clue that Dad's business was in trouble. The early 70s brought the oil crisis and a terrible recession, which hit the construction industry hard. Dad was forced to close his practice because of cash flow problems and take a job overseas. Grandma and the three of us moved to live with our extended family in Singapore.

Whispers and snide remarks about Dad and his money problems among our relatives in Singapore soon made us realise that all was not well, although Dad made no mention of his problems in his many letters and regular phone calls.

Looking back through the lens of maturity and insight, I guess the loss of his practice must have hit him hard. After years of being his own boss, he hated being an employee and soon quit. At barely 50, he suffered his first stroke. With his career and business in tatters and with bills to pay, he nevertheless chose to return to Kuala Lumpur, hoping to make a fresh start.

He took pains to keep up the façade of life being status quo whenever we visited him at our old home in suburban KL. Home was Dad's self-designed bungalow, a striking and stylish residence that has withstood the passage of time to this day.

And this was where we had the face-off with Angie, following a noisy, traditional Chinese funeral wake (which Dad would have hated as he was a thoroughly modern man) and his eventual burial in a Chinese cemetery. The funeral arrangements had been hurriedly put together by my uncles and aunts, as the three of us were making our painful, tear-stained journey back from Tioman to Kuala Lumpur.

It turned out that Dad died without leaving a will. I had no idea of the implications but I would soon find out. While my uncles and aunts argued over how best to deal with Angie's demands for money, she was busy planning her next move. It was a guerilla, stealth operation: The moment everyone had left the house, she occupied it, changed the locks and filed a police report, claiming that we had removed items from her marital home. She also invited over a couple of big, burly men who stood at the gate and aggressively told us to get lost.

It was a rude wake-up call. My innocence and trust that the world is a friendly place with good people was completely shattered. I could not believe that she would do this to us – the children of the man who had loved and sheltered her for three years! When it comes to money, I learnt that even a friend can turn enemy.

We sought the help of lawyers. One of them was sympathetic towards Angie – he took our money and did nothing. After some years of waiting, a good friend in KL introduced us to another lawyer who had more integrity. We had to go through a bewildering myriad of legal documents, overcome various obstacles and wait endlessly for all the different court processes and procedures to materialise.

In the end, 15 years after my father's death, we reached an agreement to sell the property and share a percentage of the proceeds with Angie. Being somewhat dependent on my father while living with him, she had hoped that perhaps she would at least stand to inherit something from his estate as his "common law" wife.

A common law marriage is one where the couple lives together and appears to be "married" in the eyes of friends, family and their community but never formally wed or obtain a marriage licence. They are thus difficult to prove and Angie had a weak case. Her stealth operation to wrest the property from us was done in the hope that perhaps we were too young and too weak to fight back, and that with every passing year, our exhaustion or indifference would grow, and the house would naturally be hers by default. But in the end, she caved in, simply because the house was too large and too expensive for her to maintain and she did not have the legal right to sell or lease it out.

Throughout the 15 years, there were many moments of uncertainty when I wondered if we would ever see our childhood home in KL ever again, and whether it would have been easier to just throw in the towel. Today I remember my father with a great deal of love and appreciation. But the fallout from his death cast a shadow on my young adult life. I lived, worked and played like all my peers yet I could never quite shake off the anxiety and insecurity that clung to me like a second skin from age 20 to 35 – before the cloud lifted and the sun started to shine again.

FINANCIAL LIFE LESSONS

If you are a single parent of young children, your most important act of love is to make sure that you have a will that outlines clear instructions on how you want your estate to be distributed and how you want your children to be looked after.

A will also allows you to state how you wish to make your exit – in the style that reflects your personal beliefs and values. Dad had never subscribed to Taoist beliefs yet he was given a full-blown Taoist funeral.

When there's no will, your estate will fall under the Intestacy Law, which entails additional legal procedures. They include:

- The appointment of an administrator for your estate. The administrator (who can be a close friend or family member) will have to file the "Letters of Administration"(LA), which grants the right to act on behalf of your beneficiaries. With this in hand, the final step is to file for the "Grant of Probate," which gives the right for monies to be released and distributed.

- If your estate is worth more than S$250,000 and you have minor children (below age 21), the law also requires the appointment of two guarantors, or sureties, who must each agree to guarantee the value of your estate. Why are two guarantors/sureties needed? In the eyes of the law, minors are deemed vulnerable and must be doubly protected from unscrupulous administrators who may abscond with the proceeds from the estate.

In the worst-case scenario where an administrator takes off with the money, the sureties will be liable. Just imagine: If you don't write a will, who can your orphaned children turn to? Who can they trust and appoint as their administrator? Who will step forward to be their guarantors?

The whole process – from applying for the LA to getting that all-important Grant of Probate – can take months, or in our case, years! Which brings us to the next most important point: Who will look after your children? Will your ex-spouse come to the rescue? Will he or she be the best person to care and guide your children in the way you want them to grow?

I shudder to think what could have happened to us if we didn't have grandparents and an extended family home, with uncles, aunts and cousins to provide us with food, care and shelter.

Perhaps the next most important act of love for a single parent is to have adequate life insurance coverage. The amount of life insurance should equal the grand total of yearly expenses for your children's upkeep and education, up to the time that you would expect them to graduate and start working. Insurance policies are not necessarily expensive – especially if you buy term policies with no cash value. Talk to a trusted financial adviser to determine the insurance coverage that best suits your needs.

The advantage of having life insurance is that it provides liquidity while your Grant of Probate is being filed. Under Singapore's Insurance Act, up to S$150,000 of life insurance proceeds can be disbursed on presentation of the death certificate of the deceased by the next-of-kin. Any amounts greater than S$150,000 will be distributed after the Grant of Probate is issued.

At this point, I'd like to address women who find themselves, like Angie, being the "unofficial" partner in a relationship. You could be a live-in partner, mistress or gay partner. You may feel more married than most married folks and have a connection that's made in heaven, but unfortunately, the law doesn't recognise your union. You, and the children of your union, have no natural legal rights to your partner's estate.

Facing such a dilemma, a woman has several choices. She can rely on the goodwill of her partner's family or mount a takeover like

Angie did and forever incur their wrath – not to mention years of legal wrangling.

You have a choice to speak up before it is too late. Be open to your partner about how you and/or your children would like to be financially supported if death do you part. As long as your partner is willing to put you in his will as a beneficiary, his wishes will be honoured.

Such a conversation, however, may be impossible to initiate – especially if your relationship is a clandestine one.

In my opinion, your best choice is to recognise and accept the fact that you have no legal rights to your partner's estate, and focus on building your own financial independence.

THE TRAILING SPOUSE

I met Andrea at the plush, air-conditioned lounge of a five-star hotel one scorching afternoon. An attractive woman in her early 50s with a peaches-and-cream complexion and a brilliant smile, she described herself somewhat ironically as an "Expat Wife."

Expat wife. This label, like a Louis Vuitton handbag, has come to mean so many things in an age of globalisation, where fearless business warriors and entrepreneurs from the American, European and Australian continents traverse Asia, cutting business deals and managing companies – and getting handsomely paid for it.

A local magazine, *Expat Living*, gives the rest of us an idea of a typical Expat lifestyle, with glossy pages devoted to beautiful homes, lavish holidays, extravagant entertainment and leisure pursuits. Their typical readers are the expat wives who trail after their men from one Asian city to the next. The women's jet-setting lives appear to be the stuff of dreams – Beijing, Tokyo, London, Hong Kong and so on, all cushioned by generous expat benefits and privileges.

That was the comfortable life Andrea has known for the last 30 years, as she and her young children followed her husband, Greg, from one country to the next, in his numerous job postings. "We have moved 18 times. It's always me who does the moving while my husband leaves first. I end up packing and closing everything. That has become an occupation for me over the years," she says.

It wasn't always like this for Andrea when she was younger. She had worked her way up to a specialised job in the oil and gas industry in London. Those were exciting times, Andrea recalls. "I always landed good jobs, worked hard and really enjoyed what I was doing." She laughingly described her single years as "extravagant," often dining in nice restaurants and travelling. Money was the least of her worries.

She had met Greg at work and they bonded instantly. Two years later, they were married. "He was smart and attractive, always prepared to do fun things," says Andrea. As a well-paid troubleshooter in the oil and gas industry, Greg was offered a job in Australia. Andrea, too, managed to get a job and in the early years of their marriage, with two young daughters in tow, they bought properties in the various locations they found themselves in. "We sank most of our savings in property," she recalls. Weathering the booms and busts of the era, they sometimes had to sell their property at a loss whenever a job opportunity in a new country beckoned.

Life as an expat wife was exciting, yet uncertain. Corporate nomads like Greg were faced with occasional job cuts, and always had to be nimble on their feet, keeping an eye out for their next gig. With every move, Andrea had to adjust herself to a new environment quickly. "My worst moment," Andrea notes, "was when we moved to the US and lived there for six years. It was a complete culture shock; I was very isolated and suffered from depression. It took me at least six months before I joined a support group of mothers from Australia and New Zealand and started feeling normal again." She worked part-time in the US but soon gave that up as Greg was travelling constantly and she had to care for the children.

Greg was overseas two weeks out of every month and this took a toll on their relationship. Eventually, she discovered that he had an affair while in Malaysia. She forgave him and they resolved to work on their marriage but "things were never the same," says Andrea sadly.

More job changes and more moves followed – first to Singapore and then to Japan. "Moving around really cost us; the expensive rent and the school fees especially," she says. It was the earthquake and Fukushima nuclear disaster that prompted them to move back to Singapore.

Greg worked and commuted between Singapore and Malaysia. Life fell into its usual routine until one day, out of the blue, he told her that he wanted a separation. Her eyes filling with tears, Andrea shares, "The whole thing was a bombshell. I didn't know what to do. He had this silly notion that we would live like flatmates until our younger daughter went to college. He laid down the rules for how things would work financially and how we would behave to one another."

The relationship became more and more strained until Greg gave his ultimatum: He wanted a divorce and financial settlement. Now. She would no longer have any financial access to their joint accounts. He would rent an apartment for her and their younger daughter to live in, and would support them only until their daughter finished school in two years.

After 30 years of marriage, Andrea came to the shocking realisation that most of the assets they acquired were in Greg's name. Whatever cash or assets she owned had been absorbed into the properties they had bought together over the years. There was nothing much she could do except to look for a divorce lawyer.

"If I had a career that was more portable, it would have given me enough independence to make decisions at various junctures. But when you're totally dependent on your spouse, you feel that you have to stay in a difficult marriage and for the children's sake, you decide to make the best of things," Andrea says upon reflection.

"Emotionally, you have already sacrificed quite a lot to support your spouse's career along the way. You're in a trust-based relationship and you never think that it is going to turn against you. There are things that I've learnt that I should have been more aware of. For instance, my husband never wanted me to have my own bank account.

I should have put my foot down and insisted on having my own money. I should have had an account that's just mine."

She explains, "Joint accounts are not always joint. It depends on who has control over them. You have to be careful how they are set up. He controlled the finances. That was what he wanted to do. He was very good with it. Whereas now, I realise I should have been more careful and should have played an active role with our finances because at the end of the day, you can't trust that everything is going to work out. On the other hand, what I did well was raising the children, and they've turned out to be fantastic children. I'm very proud of my daughters. I was able to spend time with them and be 100% present and involved in their lives."

Her final verdict? "Being an expat wife is a very dangerous choice to make and this applies to anyone, man or woman, who becomes a trailing spouse. You put yourself at their mercy. Every time they move, they reinvent themselves and treat it as a grand adventure, while you have to hold things together. The expectation is that you have to move with them whether you like it or not.

"So, it's a trap. You can't say 'I refuse to move'. So, you make the best of it; you quickly adapt, doing whatever you need to do to help yourself survive and help your kids settle. You have to have that total honesty and trust each other implicitly especially in Asia.

"I think my husband had a midlife crisis of sorts. Greg said, 'I want to live the second part of my life different from the first half'. When they get to this stage, they don't care what it costs them. Relationships and family become irrelevant. I'm just one case in thousands. My lawyer is handling three other cases like mine."

Despite her ordeal, Andrea credits her faith in God in keeping her cautiously optimistic about the future. She sketched for me her most ideal outcome saying, "I'd like to be extremely independent and own a business. I couldn't be in a subservient position anymore; it's being 'a nobody' in many ways. I'll be happy just to do my own thing."

FINANCIAL LIFE LESSONS

Andrea used to be an independent career woman but gave it up to devote herself to her husband and children. This is the cultural and gender norm all over the world, but how can women protect themselves from being dumped and destitute? Here are my suggestions:

1. Start financial planning when you are single

Building your wealth starts with your very first paycheck. Put 10% of your monthly pay and yearly bonuses into a savings or investment savings account and don't touch it! Raise it gradually as your pay increases. The compounding effect of interest over a long period of time is very powerful. But it only works if you save money religiously. Don't ever dip your fingers in it, except for dire emergencies. Once the emergency is over, restart.

2. Build your financial structure

Mentally name your account "My Freedom Fund" because this money is all about you. No one else. It's your future war chest. It's the money you can use perhaps 10 or 15 years down the road to embark on a personal project, be it a business, an investment, further education – anything that expands your world as an individual rather than as an extension of your husband.

As your Freedom Fund grows, consider diversifying that cash into insurance (for protection), investments (for wealth accumulation), and long-term savings (for retirement). Educate yourself about financial planning. There are many free educational resources for financial planning listed at the back of this book.

If you have started a Freedom Fund while you are young and single, it becomes a structure that you can tap on throughout your life's transitions. Want to stop work and become a full-time mum? Money in your Freedom Fund keeps compounding and may allow you to eventually do that. Husband leaves or dies? Money in your Freedom Fund is your line of defence – you'll have the financial smarts and confidence to start a new life.

3. Educate and manage

If you are already married, it's never too late to educate and upgrade your skills, get a part-time job or start a home business. Never take your eye off the ball in managing the family finances. Establish a firm footing as the family accountant and manager of your joint banking account and keep all statements and important documents filed.

4. Avoid the property trap

Never make the mistake that Andrea and Greg did of putting most of their savings into property. The problem with real estate is that it is an illiquid asset, and if you need money in a pinch, it is not so easy to sell off the property.

In a divorce, fights over property such as who owns what and who spent on what can take ages to resolve. Property prices are also sensitive to market cycles and depending on when you buy, you can either make big or lose big.

A property may look seductive but if you're paying more than you can afford by borrowing heavily, that's a flashpoint for financial disaster if you lose your job and the ability to service the loan.

MARRIED TO A MAMA'S BOY

There's a popular men's joke that goes like this: If you're on a sinking ship with your wife and mother, who would you save first? Answer: Mother. Because a man has only one mother but he can always find a new wife.

Spouses may be dispensable but mothers play a prominent role in our lives, especially in Asia. Mothers are loved and idealised because "she first loved us and gave herself to us," to paraphrase the Bible's description of the great unconditional love of Jesus for humanity.

Mothers-in-law, however, are different. They are stereotypically seen as the difficult woman who makes your life miserable. They inspire all the mother-in-law jokes that let us entertain fantasies of them meeting an untimely demise, like throwing them overboard a ship to drown.

If you ask Jocelyn, a relief teacher in her 60s, she would say that all the stereotypes about mothers-in-law are true. Jocelyn has never gotten along with her mother-in-law, Madam Tan, but she never expected that she would still be fighting with her long after the elderly woman's death!

The fight centres on an apartment owned by Jocelyn's late husband, Edward. Though the property was in his name, Madam Tan had lived there until her death. Edward, however, had neglected to mention the property in his will and now Jocelyn is locked in an ugly battle with the executors of her late mother-in-law's estate to claim the property.

Jocelyn and Edward had a happy marriage. Edward was a moderately successful self-made businessman. According to Jocelyn, he was an attentive husband who never forgot her birthday or their wedding anniversary. He would always surprise her with a holiday getaway on the latter.

But he was even more attentive to his mother, wanting to spend more and more time with her, and Jocelyn could not fathom why. "He would spend entire weekends with his mum. When he wasn't around, she would call. We would be invited to our friends' parties, weddings and birthdays, and we would always have to turn down the invitations because he had to spend time with his mother. Since we both worked, the weekend was the only time we had to catch up. I thought it was very selfish of him to insist that we spend it at her place every time," says Jocelyn.

Jocelyn was also unhappy with how Edward chose to manage their financial commitments. "He refused to give me an allowance for household expenses because I worked. When I told him that my friends' husbands gave them allowances even though they had jobs, his reply was, 'why don't you marry them?'" says Jocelyn, adding that she believed Edward was giving his mother money on the quiet.

Their family dynamics became more tense as the years went by. Jocelyn felt that she could not stop working, as she was an only child who needed to take care of her ageing parents. Her relationship with Madam Tan was cold. "My mother-in-law and sisters-in-law wanted me to be housewives like them. They couldn't understand why I had to work and disapproved of me," says Jocelyn. Giving birth to her first child, a girl, did not endear Jocelyn to Madam Tan. The matriarch, like all traditional Chinese mothers, preferred boys. She was overjoyed when Jocelyn's second child, a son, arrived, and promptly took over the babysitting.

Then one day, Madam Tan appeared at Jocelyn and Edward's doorstep ready to move in. Jocelyn was aghast. "We had agreed right from the beginning that his mother would only visit and not stay. I told him, 'This is our home. I won't have my parents coming to live with us and you won't have your parents coming to live so there won't be any friction between us.' But he chose to ignore it. He didn't control that," recalls Jocelyn angrily.

The two women clashed over the upbringing of her young son. "I wanted him to watch Sesame Street to improve his English but she ignored my wishes and let him watch whatever rubbish TV programmes he liked," says Jocelyn.

Torn between the two women in his life, Edward bought the apartment in question and assured Jocelyn that he was the sole owner. Madam Tan went to live there and according to Jocelyn, that was why her mother-in-law believed that Edward had bought the apartment for her.

The weekends at her mother-in-law's place continued and were considered sacred by Edward. "There came a time when my parents needed me more and I decided to spend more time with them during the weekends. So, Edward and I went our separate ways, only meeting when it was time to go home," recalls Jocelyn, adding that Edward did not like spending time with her parents.

It was an unusual parallel existence; a family split two ways – his and hers – with the two children divided on either side. Her son was "monopolised" by Madam Tan and was not close to his maternal grandparents while her daughter was the opposite.

"Life was comfortable but my mind wasn't free," says Jocelyn, remembering those years. Edward became ill with cancer in his 60s and though it was treated successfully, his weak heart compounded his health problems. He had a heart attack and passed away, with Jocelyn's hand in his.

According to Jocelyn, Edward's will was drawn up when he learnt that he had cancer. He had divided all his assets in equal portions to Jocelyn, their children, his mother, and his siblings. Apparently, there was more than enough to make everyone happy – except for that one apartment that Edward and his lawyer forgot about. The question is, who is the rightful owner of that apartment?

"I tried mediation as I did not want to kick her out. I even offered her half the share of the apartment but she wouldn't accept anything. Even after her death, I have to fight her estate!" exclaims Jocelyn.

Her story sounds like a long-running soap opera with no end. When I told her that it took 15 years to settle my father's estate, she retorted, "I may not even be alive if it takes that long!"

As for her two children, she doesn't expect them to show the same devotion that she and Edward had for their parents. Growing up split between two camps, her children seldom call and their relationship with her is strained.

"Gone are the days when your children will take care of you. My friends say the same thing. All women have to understand basic finance to survive on their own," concludes Jocelyn sadly.

FINANCIAL LIFE LESSONS

Be aware that when you marry, you are not only marrying your spouse but his entire family, warts and all! If you feel uneasy or uncomfortable with your in-laws, pay attention – it's a red alert for problems ahead.

This story illustrates a clash of family values: Edward came from a traditional Chinese family where the matriarch is revered, respected and adored. In a traditional Chinese family, males are held in higher regard than females. Women are not expected to work or to have a life of their own, but to devote themselves to the family. Daughters-in-law must accept their place as outsiders in the family and must always defer to the matriarch or mother-in-law.

Jocelyn, an only child, grew up with a completely different set of values. She was taught to speak up and to question – behaviors that were not acceptable to her husband and her in-laws.

This creates a constant tug of war and tension between different priorities: Edward's duty towards his mother versus his duty towards his wife; Jocelyn's duty towards her own parents versus her duty towards her mother-in-law.

When it comes to money, a clash of values spells trouble in a marriage. Who comes first? Where does love end and duty begin?

In the normal line of inheritance law, the spouse and children come first, followed by parents and siblings. However, it appears that Edward probably found himself torn between both sides, and he must have decided that the fairest course of action was to divide his estate equally among his family members.

He could have genuinely forgotten to include the apartment in his will, or he could have "forgotten" on purpose. When we face a dilemma, the natural response is to delay making a decision because we don't want to face the consequences of siding with either of the opposing parties.

If this was a sinking ship, Edward would have started swimming and let the two women fight for the life raft!

It is too late for Edward and Jocelyn to turn back the clock but how can we prevent our family relationships from unravelling? Here are some points:

1. Have a frank conversation

Discuss your expectations with your spouse and work towards a common purpose.

2. Be prepared to negotiate and compromise

If you can't stand your in-laws but must tolerate them, work out a compromise with your spouse to see them only occasionally in a more meaningful way (like helping to cook) rather than torture yourself with an obligatory weekly visit.

3. Seek professional help

Do not bottle up unhappy feelings but seek family therapy if necessary. Jocelyn and Edward's situation could have been prevented from getting worse if they had been willing to talk it over with a counsellor. Do not live in denial.

4. Make your final intentions clear

Edward could have signed over the apartment to his mother before his death and given the rest of his estate to Jocelyn and the children. Or, he could have put all his assets into a trust to benefit all his family members fairly. There are different ways of distributing your assets. Be aware that dividing everything equally among all your family members may not work and may lead to potential disputes as this story illustrates.

PART 2:

Breaking Through

I AM THE CAPTAIN OF MY SOUL

"**I** am the master of my fate, I am the captain of my soul."

These words from the poem Invictus by William Henley hold special meaning for May Lee. She would read the lines whenever she feels defeated and depressed, and remind herself that she can conquer whatever trials and tribulations that may come her way.

Single, articulate and attractive with long jet-black hair, it's hard to imagine May Lee as defeated and depressed. Yet, she has weathered more trials in the last 10 years than most people have over a lifetime.

May Lee came of age in the 1990s when the economy was booming and life was just one long party. She was lavishly pampered by her doting parents and spent her early 20s slacking off, drifting into a brief marriage followed by a quickie divorce. "Money was meaningless to me – I could buy a $600 top and not feel the pinch," recalls May Lee ruefully.

She had a desire to make a difference in the world and her friends saw her as a "champagne socialist" but nothing she did, such as dabbling in freelance writing and running a small business, was done with the intention of making or saving money. "You could say I was either a dreamer or rebel," says May Lee with a laugh.

However, she knew she had to get out of her partying ways. "I realised that my parents were not as financially secure as I had imagined. Money was tight, we weren't having our lavish dinners anymore, and it was time for me to grow up," says May Lee.

So, she decided to go to London to take up a master's degree in Oriental Studies. "I promised myself that I was going to be very responsible and get a good job, regardless of whether I was going to like it or not. I wasn't sure what kind of job. I even toyed with the idea of staying on in London but I didn't have any money left to continue living in the very expensive city."

London turned out to be both exciting and painful. She had to juggle the demands of her studies and deal with her heartbreak over a broken relationship. It caused her to become a two pack-a-day smoker. "I was smoking like a chimney just to get through the day. Most of my money went into cigarettes – the equivalent of about $30 Singapore dollars per day. The rest of the money went to counselling. I was so depressed that my friends couldn't bear to be near me anymore!" says May Lee.

She was struggling to finish her dissertation and also losing weight drastically. She attributed her weight loss to stress and her smoking, but it was actually much more sinister. After completing her studies, she returned to Singapore still nursing a broken heart and looking for a job. "I was alone at home one day and decided to check my breasts for lumps, as I had just spoken to my sister about it. My knuckle hit something that felt hard and then blood started spurting out from my nipples, staining the sofa," recalls May Lee.

Scared and worried, she immediately went to her doctor who referred her to an oncologist. More tests followed. She remembers her mammogram vividly, "There was blood all over the place. I was terrified and horrified." A biopsy later confirmed the dreaded prognosis: Stage 4 breast cancer. The oncologist ordered an immediate mastectomy followed by chemotherapy, and told her that she would have to be on hormonal drugs for the long haul.

She smoked her last cigarette and had her mastectomy. She then endured months of painful chemotherapy treatments, which left her nauseous, bald, bloated and constipated. "I had always been vain and taken great pride in my appearance but now I couldn't even bear to look at myself in the mirror! I was fat and bald, and had red scars all over my body from the chemo drugs that were injected into my veins. I had another big red scar under my arm because my lymph nodes were removed."

Having cancer not only drained her emotionally, but financially as well. She had a critical illness insurance policy with a very small sum assured, which barely covered all her medical bills. "I made the mistake of buying the policy and not reading the fine print, and forgetting what I bought. My insurer refused to cover certain treatments such as breast reconstruction and, in the end, my parents and I had to cough up quite a bit of money. It really ate into my parents' savings," says May Lee.

After her treatment was over, she was ready to face the world again. But the emotional scars remained. "I still hated to look at myself and I didn't want to face my friends," she says. Escaping seemed to be the best option and so she took off for Beijing and enrolled herself in a Mandarin course for international students, with the hope of eventually working in China. "I wanted a fresh start but I still felt lousy about myself and moving to a new country didn't change how I felt," she observes.

Following a stint as a magazine editor, she found a job with an international hotel chain in Beijing that seemed to be an answer to all her financial problems. It offered an attractive expat package and she could also save money by having her meals at the hotel. However, working in a hotel was a mixed blessing. "After a while, I found the work to be pretty mindless but it allowed me to bury myself away from the world because I didn't want to deal with how ugly I looked. I gained more weight because I was caught up in a vicious cycle of long working hours and late meals," she recalls.

She also hung on because she had started to experience excruciating back pain. Terrified that it was her cancer recurring, she went into denial, refusing to see the doctor and bearing the pain as bravely as she could. "I had no more money left for any medical treatments and decided to hold on until I had passed my probation period with the hotel, so that I would be covered by our employee insurance," she explains.

The pain wouldn't go away. Seeking relief, she went to a traditional healer who twisted her body this way and that. The next day, she couldn't get out of bed and was rushed to hospital in a stretcher. An MRI confirmed that it wasn't cancer but a ruptured disc that had affected a crucial nerve in her spinal column. If she wasn't operated on immediately, she would be paralysed. The surgeon secured four titanium screws in her spine. This time, the medical bill was 250,000 RMB (S$50,000), which was fortunately covered by her employee insurance.

"Till today, I'm very grateful that my employer paid every cent and came to my rescue but that didn't make me love my job any more," says May Lee. She worked for a few more years with the hotel but her dissatisfaction and depression grew. She dared not take the chance to leave because she did not have any insurance coverage.

"I've been cancer-free for more than 10 years now yet every insurance company I go to has denied me coverage," says May Lee bitterly. "I suppose, if I had bought a policy that gave me peace of mind, I would have left my job long ago to do other things," she adds. Her burnout reached such a critical point that she found it impossible to carry on and asked for a leave of absence.

"I came back to Singapore and really worked on myself with a life coach to sort out all the emotional pain that I was hiding and the wall that I had built around myself since getting cancer," says May Lee.

Then a friend who's a senior manager of a reinsurance company helped her by introducing her to an insurer who was willing to cover her against all major illnesses including the recurrence of her cancer. The premium was hefty – USD7,000 per year, with an annual increase of 10%.

It was money that she was prepared to pay, as it brought her the peace of mind to look for another job – this time in Singapore. "I think the whole process of regaining my self-confidence and dignity to become empowered again started when I quit my job," says May Lee. She experienced her first breakthrough when a heritage foundation hired her as a consultant to promote a historical landmark in Malaysia – a project that is close to her heart.

Today, May Lee is healthy and works at a job she loves and which also fulfills her need to make a difference. "I've learnt to accept myself as I am. I know that I can never regain the body I once had, or make back all the money I've lost, but I'm doing what I can to get to a better place," she reflects.

She is finally, the Captain of Her Soul.

FINANCIAL LIFE LESSONS

May Lee's story highlights some important lessons:

1. Review your insurance regularly

You may have "outgrown" the first insurance policy you ever bought, due to a rise in your income and responsibilities. A $25,000 insurance coverage may be all you need at age 21. At 40 years old, however, your income needs (with inflation) would have increased many times, making that insurance cover insufficient.

Insurance companies are also constantly introducing new benefits, improvements and enhancements to their products. You will be losing out if you don't keep updated.

If May Lee had kept herself updated, she would have found out about the following innovations introduced in the last 10 years. They include:

- Women's Critical Illness Cover: These types of policies cover major illnesses that are exclusive to women such as women's cancers and others. They also include benefits not found in other policies such as breast reconstruction after a mastectomy
- Early Stage Illness Cover and Multiple Illness Cover: These policies are designed to protect you from multiple illnesses as well as a recurrence of your major illness
- Integrated MediShield Plans and MediShield Life: These schemes form the backbone of Singapore's national health insurance plan for citizens and permanent residents, offering whole life coverage for hospitalisation. MediShield Life, introduced in 2015, also covers pre-existing illnesses

2. Plan your insurance coverage carefully

Seek guidance from your financial adviser and know what you're buying. It's like packing the right parachute. The right time to check your parachute is when you're on the ground. No point checking it when you're out of the plane because it'll be too late.

In May Lee's case, she was turned down by all insurance companies after having cancer, as she was considered to have a "pre-existing" condition. To obtain insurance again, she had to pay a much higher premium.

3. Employee insurance ends when you leave the company

Your company insurance plan is rarely portable. Fear of losing her insurance kept May Lee stuck in a job she disliked.

If you have a serious pre-existing medical condition, resigning and then starting a new job puts you at risk again. You are likely to be put under probation with no insurance benefits and even if you pass the probation period, your new insurer may require a waiting period before they insure your pre-existing condition.

MINISTER OF HOME AFFAIRS

S haron reminds me of the women in my family – neat, hardworking and conservative hands-on working mums who run their households like well-oiled machines. She also reminds me of all the executive secretaries I know who are strictly no-nonsense, always reliable, unruffled and discreet.

But Sharon is far from average. Although she doesn't make any waves or trumpet her cause, Sharon is a solo crusader for desperate women – women who have fallen on hard times because of errant husbands and widowhood. She personally guides and encourages them to pick themselves up and find solutions to overcome their problems.

It is something that she enjoys doing apart from her full-time job as a personal secretary to a company director because she can identify with what these women are going through. She herself was similarly adrift in desperate circumstances 10 years ago when her husband died suddenly at age 51, leaving her with a pile of loans and three young school-going children.

"My husband was the 'Minister of Home Affairs'; he handled all the bills and I was only responsible for looking after the kids, going to work, and paying for the maid," recalls Sharon. "I didn't really have to worry about the household. I worked to earn my own keep because I didn't come from a well-off family and I always wanted to have a job so that I could be self-sufficient."

The way that they handled their finances was typical of most Singapore couples. They had a joint account and owned an HDB flat, split 50-50 in both their names. Her husband, a sales and marketing manager, took up insurance policies for himself and their children, while she had her own bank account and insurance policies. He didn't write a will because he thought it was unnecessary. They never discussed the details of their finances with each other.

Sharon was vaguely aware that her husband had started a small sideline business with his friends, but she chose not to ask any questions. "After he died, I decided to look through his big pile of papers and realised that there were various business loans to be paid up, in the region of $80,000, from different banks.

"His papers were all in a mess and I was like, 'What do I do, where to start, who to start paying, and how do I know if it's genuine?' He didn't keep any proper records and, sad to say, as a secretary, I should have known better and helped him to file his things, but I did not bother," admits Sharon.

She dumped all the papers in a box and stuffed them in the storeroom. "My priority was to make sure the children were alright. They were in a state of shock. My youngest was just seven when her father died and she took it very hard because she was Daddy's darling. It would have taken me ages to sort through the pile and the kids had to come first. I decided that the best action to take was to sit back and let the banks come after me," she recalls.

Sure enough, the letters started arriving, one by one, polite reminders to pay up. As her husband had died intestate (without a will), even their joint bank account was frozen. Fortunately, Sharon had always believed in saving at least one year's salary in her own bank account for emergencies and her husband had an insurance policy that she was able to claim.

Says Sharon, "My job trained me to prioritise. I approached my children's schools and asked their teachers to help keep an eye on them – text me, call me to let me know how they are doing or if they need counselling. I told my kids to approach their teachers if they needed any help. Once that was sorted out, I felt that I could tackle other issues."

She took the banks' letters to a law firm and engaged them to act on her behalf. Months passed and still the letters kept coming. To her alarm, the interest on the loans kept accruing and the principal amount got bigger and bigger.

Her lawyer assured her that they were working on her case and to be patient. But Sharon's unease grew when she received a letter informing her that a caveat had been lodged by a bank: "I didn't even know what a caveat was. How would I know whether there were other caveats? I called the bank but they told me that they would only speak to my lawyer," says Sharon, describing her frustration at the time.

Fed up with her lawyer, she called the Subordinate Court and was directed to an external legal aid service bureau which duly did a search on the caveats filed. She was told to expect more caveats. A caveat is a legal warning giving notice of the bank's right to take action against the borrower. Meanwhile, she was receiving threatening phone calls from the banks' debt collectors. "I told them, 'I want to pay and move on with my life but you're not working out a solution!' They kept insisting that they would only talk to my lawyer, which made me realise that they were more frightened to see me than I was of them. It wasn't me who owed them the money but my husband so, what could they do to me?" recalls Sharon.

The feisty widow decided to take a radical approach and wrote to the CEO or Chairman of the banks to explain her plight. "It was very easy to Google their names. If the CEO was Singaporean, it might work, I told myself. If I looked at the person's face and the CEO didn't look like the sympathetic sort, I would write directly to the Chairman. I wrote very personal letters, explaining that I was doing my best to pay up, but all I kept getting was rudeness and threats from their staff.

I appealed for a workable solution and time to repay the loans," said Sharon.

A glimmer of hope came when the legal department of one of the banks called her to arrange for a meeting. Says Sharon, "As a secretary, I know that if an order comes from the top, things will start moving. If I had approached the legal department directly, they would have ignored me." The other banks followed suit, and she was able to bring all of them to the negotiating table to work out an installment payment plan for discharging the loans. "They could not write off the loans completely because they had to comply with MAS (Monetary Authority of Singapore) rules. But I realised that I shouldn't worry myself mad to pay up. The loans were my husband's; they had nothing to do with me. So, I asked them if they would accept a token sum to the best of my ability. If the amount was big, I would ask them to stop the interest. I said to them, 'I will pay; give me time to pay. If the interest goes up and I die from stress, you get nothing. At least if I'm alive and working, I'll pay.' They laughed, but to me it's simple logic."

Within a week or two, Sharon had successfully negotiated with each bank to pay only a percentage of the loans in monthly installments. Before that, she had marched to her erstwhile lawyer's office to demand a refund of her deposit and to discharge them from acting on her behalf.

"If I had stuck with the lawyer, I would definitely have had to pay 100% of the loans and interest, and pay the law firm another $5,000 to $8,000 to get my husband's estate settled," says Sharon. With her lawyer discharged, the banks had no choice but to deal with her directly.

But she faced another uphill task of settling the rest of her husband's estate. She went back to the legal service bureau and began the tedious process of filing for the Letters of Administration from scratch, with helpful guidance from the staff. It involved filling up "thousands of forms, queuing up for hours in court just to pay stamp duty, and a lot of running around," recalls Sharon, adding that her handbag was her constant companion, always packed with all the original and photocopies of her and her husband's IDs, his death certificate, their children's birth certificates, and other legal documents she carried everywhere she went.

It took another eight months before a probate was issued – a licence for the discharge of all assets belonging to her late husband. Throughout the whole process, Sharon kept the children updated on everything. They even accompanied her to court. "I felt it was important for the whole family to know that we were in this together," says Sharon. "I wanted them to know that money is important, and that we need to be hands-on in managing it," she adds.

One traumatic event can change one's life forever. For Sharon and her children, it has strengthened them and made them more independent. The family copes without a domestic helper – all the children take turns to do household chores and are able to prepare their own meals.

Aware of the strain of providing for all three on her single income, Sharon is not embarrassed to tap all the financial aid resources available for their education. Her eldest son has since graduated from university and has a good job, and both her daughters are undergraduates.

Sharon has started paying it forward by helping women caught up in similar circumstances, coaching them and offering these women advice and guidance. "If my husband had managed his finances better, I wouldn't be what I am today. I wouldn't be so driven with my mission to help others," she reflects. Indeed, in her own quiet way, Sharon has become the Minister of Home Affairs whom many women can thank.

FINANCIAL LIFE LESSONS

Sharon admits that her greatest mistake was not paying attention to how her husband was managing his financial affairs. This is a common problem among many couples who maintain a joint account, as well as a "His" and "Her" account.

The root of the problem lies in being uncomfortable discussing money with each other. If you came from a family where money is never discussed openly, you tend to bury your head in the sand like an ostrich when money issues arise.

You may think, "If everything is okay, why rock the boat? I can trust my husband to do the right thing because he's a family man." Women dare not ask questions for fear of being perceived as obsessed with money, naggy, or worse, coming across as not trusting their men.

I remember an incident years ago when I was in a serious relationship and contemplating marriage. When I questioned my then-boyfriend about paying a utility bill, he became very angry and defensive. My response was to shut up in order to preserve the harmony of our relationship. I believe I'm not the only one who hates confrontation with our loved ones over money. It leaves you guilt-ridden with a bad taste in your mouth.

Sharon's response was to save one year's salary in her bank account – just in case. She told me that her husband's job involved lots of entertaining and being surrounded by women. She was thus always mindful about her own money and wanted to be secure – in case he falls for another woman and walks out.

But as her experience shows, whatever your husband does with his money can affect your financial peace of mind and have serious consequences for the family. So, what should couples do? Here are my suggestions:

1. Pre-marital workshops

Before you marry, sign up for a couples retreat and workshop where your expectations about marriage, religion, sex, money, parenting, and career are openly explored and discussed under the guidance of professional marriage counsellors. It is the best investment you'll ever make. It will also set the foundation for how you would communicate with each other during marriage.

This is the time to be honest with one another, iron out differences, and be aware of potential problems. If the workshop reveals that the gulf between you and your partner is too wide, you'll save yourself a lot of trouble and heartbreak by not going through with the marriage.

I know this sounds harsh and not very romantic. But think of the expenditure on weddings these days – the wedding dinner, the photography and outfits – only to end in disaster! A former colleague of mine had the most lavish wedding but six months later, her marriage crashed because she found out that her husband was a habitual borrower and gambler.

2. Monthly financial review

If you are already married, make it a point to have a monthly financial review with your spouse. This is when you review the family budget and discuss any major financial decisions you plan to make, such as buying a car or property, or starting a business.

3. Solvency review

Review your current debt obligations before taking on more debt. One way to find out if you may have difficulty repaying the loan is to divide your total loan quantum by your total income. As a rule of thumb, your loans must not be more than 50% of your total income.

4. Annual review

Besides monthly reviews, couples should set medium and long-term financial goals and review them annually with their financial and investment adviser.

5. Mind your husband's business

Be aware of his friends, business associates and partners. Your husband may have established financial ties or signed agreements with people who may not be trustworthy. Use your woman's intuition to discern if an associate or business agreement is genuine. Sometimes it takes a second pair of eyes to scrutinise a contract and pick out the flaws. If you and your husband have established yourselves as a team, he will trust your judgement.

6. Keep updated records

Maintain separate and proper files for all your important papers, especially your insurance policies, bank loans and will. When a person dies, the first duty of his executor is to compile a proper accounting of the deceased person's assets. Don't leave your papers in a mess for your poor executor to sort through!

7. Make a will

Sharon emerged a stronger person after sorting through her late husband's mess. She had to deal with the banks, the paperwork and the long hours of queuing just to get his estate discharged. It took more than a year. In my case, it took 15 years! Wouldn't you prefer to spare your spouse and children the trouble? Both husband and wife must thus write a will.

THE POWER OF GIVING

Justine has always been independent and made her own decisions. Meeting her for the first time, I was immediately struck by her confident, forthright and breezy manner. She welcomed me into her home office in an elegant bungalow tastefully decorated with plants, artworks and family pictures.

Here is a woman who is in control of her life and seems to have it all, I thought. However, I soon learnt that this indomitable lady had recently fought two major battles that almost broke her spirit, but, thankfully, did not.

Justine's business is jewellery design – producing one-of-a-kind, artisanal pieces that are sold through private shows and exclusive boutiques in Singapore, Malaysia and Bali. Being an entrepreneur runs in her genes. "Back home in the US, everyone in my family did their own thing – my grandfather and Dad ran their own companies; my mother was an interior designer and real estate agent," shares Justine.

At 25, after working as a graphic designer for a few years, Justine and her friend started their own design company. "We worked out of a closet in my dad's office," she says. Their design business grew and they added a public relations division. She was able to sell the two businesses at a profit before coming to Singapore with her former husband.

Six months after arriving in Singapore, Justine found herself pregnant with twins. "I had put off having children for a long time because I wanted to make sure that I was financially independent," she says. She spent the next three to four years being a full-time mum and expat wife. "I love my kids and being a mum but it wasn't enough," she recalls. During a visit to India with her mother, she met a jewellery manufacturer who was looking to sell his pieces in Singapore.

She bought the jewellery pieces and her creative mind was reawakened. "I realised that I really missed the process of design. I started cutting up the stones, creating concepts and managed to put together a small collection," says Justine. It was snapped up by the stores and the success of her new venture gave her the confidence to buy more stones and create more designs. Her business in Singapore was born. "It wasn't a huge business but it was enough to sustain my needs and pay my bills," says Justine, who had always believed that women should have their own money.

While her business was doing well, storm clouds were brewing in her marriage. "I wanted to get out of my marriage for all the right reasons and that's when you have to look at your life as a divorced expat female in Singapore and all the financial struggle that comes with it," she confides. She started the uphill task of untangling and separating her finances from her husband's.

"I did a lot of research on the law and the Women's Charter, and how you can protect yourself. I strongly believe that women in a divorce need to do their homework and play it as a chess game two to three steps ahead of their husbands in order to survive in this country. If you don't, and if your ex-husband gets angry and decides to cut you off, even in a legal divorce, they are not obliged to divide their assets fairly.

"You can't imagine going down this route after you've been married for over 20 years but I've seen it happen more times than not, to expat wives. The husband usually wants to hurt the wife financially by cutting off support, selling properties she's not aware of, and moving money around," she says.

Fortunately, after more than 10 years living in Singapore, Justine and her husband had become permanent residents, which gave her more rights than an expat wife on a Dependant's Pass. She was able to withdraw her share of money from their joint account and also remove his name as co-signatory of her business account. She packed her bags and left with her children.

"I got a cheap apartment and didn't know if I might meet the rent from month to month. But I knew I had to do what I had to do. I knew I had enough to sustain myself and the kids," she recalls. That knowledge gave her the will and focus to move forward with the divorce. Because she had done her homework, Justine, her ex-husband and their mediator were able to "decouple" their finances smoothly in one day without going to court.

"My divorce only cost $20,000 when it normally would have cost $40,000 to $50,000. I got what I thought was fair, which was maintenance for the children and their education. Arguing over the rest of the money wasn't worth it because at the end of the day, which is more important: money or your happiness? So, I pretty much let go of everything except for the children's maintenance."

Following her divorce, Justine worked "like a mad woman" pouring all her energy into her business. She worked from home while taking care of her twins – a son and daughter – and being their driver, cook, maid and homework tutor all rolled into one. She lost 30kg but her business was thriving, with orders for her jewellery coming from resorts all over the region and as far as Aspen, Colorado in the US. She also met, fell in love and moved in with her current partner.

Then life threw her another unexpected punch, this time a stab through the heart. Her young son Steve became seriously ill with Stage 4 lymphoma two years ago. It was just too much for Justine to bear. Seeking treatment for Steve in the best children's cancer hospital in the US, she let go of her business, said goodbye to her partner, packed up her house and sent her daughter to live with her best friend.

Steve's medical expenses were astronomical. Treatment in Singapore and the US cost S$350,000 and US$3 million respectively. Although a large part of the cost was covered by her ex-husband's insurance (including a policy that he had bought for Steve when he was a baby), it was not enough. To top it all, their US healthcare insurer was reluctant to pay and they almost lost the coverage. There were also all the extraordinary expenses that insurance would not cover such as 24-hour nursing, health supplements and counselling for emotional support.

Her friends rallied, organising a fundraiser "so I wouldn't be destitute on the streets." They even headed committees to make sure that her daughter was looked after and her house was cleaned regularly while she was away.

Though she had vowed never to allow herself to be financially dependent on anyone, all that Justine had now was money trickling in from the sales of her dwindling jewellery merchandise, maintenance from her ex-husband, and help from her parents and partner. "I was really moved and shocked by the extent of human kindness that allowed me to focus 100 percent on my battle," says Justine.

Sadly, Steve succumbed to the cancer and passed away in 2014 at the tender age of 14. "It has been a long road recovering from his death and getting back on my feet again," admits Justine. She is restarting her business with a new jewellery collection but somehow senses that her passion is being re-directed.

"I'm writing a book to help survivors of cancer and their caregivers – a book that, I hope, will bring insights into how hospitals and families can work together. My passion is now in giving. Making money is secondary. I want to talk to doctors about holistic care, from the perspective of parents and patients.

"I'm not sure if my book will overhaul the healthcare system, but at least I hope it can change our mindset about healthcare. I'm going to give tips on how patients and caregivers can find strength by tapping on the support of their community and their religion, and how to take care of themselves rather than rely solely on drugs and medical treatments alone," says Justine.

For Justine, financial freedom is no longer about accumulating wealth mindlessly. She has spent a lifetime minding her business and designing her own success. Now, she's ready to face a new chapter.

FINANCIAL LIFE LESSONS

Here's what we can all learn from Justine's experience:

1. Financial confidence

Justine demonstrated a sense of confidence that very few young women have at age 25. She knew what she was good at; she knew her strengths and her ability to start a business and make money.

She had already started building a "Freedom Fund" (remember Andrea's story in Chapter 2?) long before she married consisting of her business, savings and investments. Having a financial structure allowed her to take a hiatus when she married and started her family. It gave her the confidence to drop her business when her son fell ill even though she faced enormous bills. She knew that she could always resume her business again.

2. Being mindful of her expenses

Justine started her business with low overheads using her dad's office. Some entrepreneurs like the trappings of success such as the big office and expensive address more than they like to work at their business. Success is about starting small before growing big.

3. Pursuit of passion

It is not money that drives Justine but her passion. She had a passion for design and creativity that she fully expressed through her business – first graphic design then jewellery. Financial freedom is a goal that starts by asking yourself a few questions: What are you good at? What are you passionate about? What are the strengths you have that will help you make money to live the life you want?

4. The ability to make hard choices

Too many women stay in bad marriages for the sake of their young children, not realising that a dysfunctional marriage is even more detrimental to a child and teenager's emotional development, and may affect their ability to form healthy relationships. Justine did not try to hang on to a failing marriage. She faced reality, did her homework, and was "two to three steps" ahead of her ex-husband in protecting her financial assets when her marriage fell apart.

5. Importance of making friends and paying forward

Justine developed a circle of close friends who were more than willing to help her when her son fell ill. Too many women remain cloistered within their own comfort zones, feeling that they cannot trust people outside their immediate circle. But the truth is, good friendships always outlast marriages.

Start by developing your own network of friends by joining networking groups, "mumpreneur" groups and other interest groups. You never know when you may need their help. Reciprocate their support by paying forward – help someone else in need.

6. Learn from loss

The loss of a business and the loss of a child are tragic, but it is not the end of you. Give yourself a time out to grieve all you want and lick your wounds. Get professional help if necessary, then pick yourself up and face a fresh chapter.

PART 3:

Growing and Becoming

LEARNING NEVER STOPS

Thin may be beautiful, but Julia has a heart for women who struggle with their weight, as she herself often has. After a long career as a lawyer, she decided to step off the corporate treadmill at the age of 48 to pursue her interest in psychotherapy, specialising in helping women to overcome their eating disorders and body image issues.

"I never seriously thought about retirement or even planned for it, but when I hit my mid 40s, I realised that the rush that I used to get from my job – where every cell in my body was tuned into figuring out the next big business opportunity – that drive was gone," says Julia, referring to her work as a trust lawyer in a bank.

It was around this time that her employer sent her for a course in investor behaviour and psychology that proved to be a turning point. "It was an eye-opener for me when I realised that psychology plays such a big role in our behaviour and motivation, and I was hooked!" She signed up for a psychology degree course in a local college, completed it, and has since embarked on her "rebirth" as a therapist.

"I'm not looking to make half a million dollars a year – I'm perfectly happy making just $3,000 a month to cover my expenses," says Julia about her second career. She acknowledges that it's a far cry from her previous life where she was head of department earning – yes – half a million dollars a year.

Chasing money has never been her style, though money was important when she was growing up. She recalls, "I didn't grow up in a well-off family; my father was a habitual gambler and risk-taker who loved going to the casino and traded recklessly in the stock market. My parents argued constantly about money so from a very young age, I realised its value even before I had any."

Her parents were too cash-strapped to send her to university so Julia, an average student, did what most young ladies did in the 1980s – she went to secretarial school. "I realised very early on that in order to acquire wealth, I needed to earn it through a salaried job and the perks that came with it," she says.

She worked as a personal secretary in the legal department of a large bank and discovered that she had a competitive advantage. "I wrote better memos than everyone else. I love to read, I love learning, and this opened many doors for me because I never sold myself short and always looked for ways to use my strengths in my job," she says. Her boss suggested that she study for a Bachelor of Law (LLB) from the University of London, which she acquired through distance learning and evening classes.

Julia took on the challenge with her characteristic pragmatic approach to life. "Although I love to read and write, I didn't want to stress myself out studying to achieve high distinction – it was OK for me to aim just to pass with a 'C' and qualify as a lawyer," she says. She attended classes faithfully and ploughed through the course for the next few years, finally getting her degree in her late 20s while still working as a secretary.

Her pragmatism also led her to assess her skills realistically after getting her degree. "To be a lawyer, I needed to achieve first-class honours and have very good results, otherwise I'd end up working for a small firm with low pay and few opportunities," she says. A friend suggested that with her banking background, she would do very well in trust law. With the liberalisation of financial regulations, banks in the late 1990s were beginning to act as trustees for other financial institutions, and trust law became an open field with few players.

Julia found herself at the right place at the right time. Her legal department was absorbed into a much bigger bank with important trust clients and she found herself at the centre of the action. It wasn't long before she was at the top of her game, managing her own department, jetting around the world to meet clients, and earning a six-figure salary with perks to match. She had well and truly left the secretarial pool and was soaring. She also met and married her soulmate who is just as successful.

If this sounds like the stuff of fairy tales of a woman living a charmed life, Julia is quick to dispel the notion. "My friends have said that I'm a very lucky person but I think that everyone is lucky – it all comes down to whether you can see and seize the opportunity if it presents itself," she asserts.

Her work ethic was a factor in her success, too. "Whatever I do, I provide value. Most people tend to draw lines and say 'this is not my job' but I always end up doing a lot more than my actual job scope because I saw my role as helping my boss achieve her own KPIs. It enabled me to have a wider perspective beyond my immediate job. I became an all-rounder and seen as someone who had a lot more knowledge than the average employee."

Julia has also never gotten into a fight or an argument with anyone in her career. "I have many friends because I don't hold grudges, take things to heart or burn bridges with anyone, even when they try to hurt me. No emotional meltdowns. I always maintain a neutral stance because you never know when you may run into this person again.

"The difference between men and women in the corporate world is that men can go for drinks after a fight but women will let the bad feelings simmer and hold a grudge. I just let it go. Any bad feelings I have about a person get dissipated very quickly. I suppose this was how I survived office politics," she says with a laugh.

The former secretary, C-grade student, and high-flying corporate lawyer has now achieved the goal that many dream of but few achieve:

"retirement" before the age of 55. With her own investment portfolio and a property that brings in passive income, she can afford to take it easy. But the conventional picture of wealthy retirement – playing golf, endless vacations, planning charity fundraisers and shopping for designer toys – holds little attraction for Julia.

"My work was a big part of me; it was my life and my identity but when I left my job, I lost the prestige of having a position and a name card," she admits. Her reputation as a trust lawyer is such that she could still have her old job and salary back if she wants to, but she chooses not to. Again, it's her financial independence achieved after years of hard work that gives her this luxury of choice. There's also something else: her newfound passion for helping women who are lonely and lost. She says, "Being a psychotherapist and helping women live healthier lives with more confidence is now my mission. I can see myself doing this for a long, long time, up to my old age."

FINANCIAL LIFE LESSONS

The term "mid-life crisis" has become a cliché, referring to one's overall dissatisfaction with life as we approach middle age. We often say people are having a mid-life crisis when they leave their jobs, their marriages and their families at a certain age – usually after 40.

Today, the middle-aged are not the only ones in crisis: 25- and 30-year-olds are also experiencing a "quarter-life crisis" characterised by not knowing what career path to follow and feelings of being lost and adrift in this cold hard world.

Julia did not go through a quarter-life crisis when she was young or a mid-life crisis when she hit her forties. She simply took the most practical and available job that she could find (be a secretary) and mastered it – steadily building up knowledge and experience until she became a lawyer herself.

Having successfully transitioned from secretary to lawyer, she was able to navigate her transition from lawyer to psychotherapist with equal confidence – even the loss of income and position is secondary next to her new passion. What can we learn from Julia?

1. Opportunities are everywhere

Building wealth and financial independence starts with a commitment to a goal. Julia knew that in order to get out of her family's cycle of not having enough, she had to do her very best *where she was.* Opportunities are waiting at every turn, for the best person to grab them.

It means ignoring quick fixes and pipe dreams like winning the lottery or marrying a millionaire. It means working smart, mastering your job, and learning to understand every aspect of your company's product, service and business – even if you are in an entry-level or junior position. Imagine yourself in the shoes of your boss or the founder of your company. What are his concerns? How can you address these concerns and add value in the job that you are doing? Identify the opportunities that allow you to grow and move forward.

2. Relationships matter

Mentors are very important in your wealth-building journey. So are business associates and co-workers. Julia credits her EQ (emotional intelligence) in her willingness to seek and accept advice and her refusal to be controlled by negative emotions, as factors in her success.

3. No short cuts

Julia invested time to educate herself – first as a lawyer and later as a psychotherapist. It took several years of learning on-the-job and cultivating relationships and knowledge while slogging for a degree before she earned her ultimate reward and financial independence.

Are there any shortcuts to earning your first million, buying your dream home or becoming a wealthy investor like Warren Buffett? The answer is "No." Don't be fooled by the numerous wealth "gurus" out there who promise to sell you their formula for instant wealth. People who follow their "too good to be true" advice end up getting badly hurt.

Read the story of Warren Buffett and you'll realise that even the richest man in the world learned all about wealth and finance through education and his early experience as a newspaper delivery boy! Wealth comes from discipline and patience.

4. Retirement means doing something you love

What do you do after you've reached your financial goals? You reflect and set new goals that connect with a higher purpose and higher self, as Julia has done.

Don't view life as a linear trajectory to infinity but as an open field, with paths to explore and opportunities to use your talents and give back. Your expertise in one profession can open doors to people and markets that badly need your gifts – perhaps in a different capacity and role.

Famous Hollywood actress Jane Fonda is one woman who has gone through more transitions than any public figure I know. She was a movie star and sex symbol in her 20s, an anti-war protester in her 30s, a successful businesswoman and exercise guru in her 40s, and a social activist in her later years. Now in her 70s, she delivered a moving talk at a TEDxWomen 2011 event in which she urged her audience to celebrate their "Third Act," where "age becomes potential not pathology." What are the dreams hidden in you that you have yet to explore? How can you use your financial independence to transition into your very own Third Act?

TAMING THE DEBT MONSTER

Getting your first paycheck and your first credit card is a heady experience for most 20-somethings. When I was in my early 20s, I remember feeling that sense of power when I held my first Visa credit card, knowing that it could buy me that dream outfit, vacation, designer watch, bag and indeed, anything I wished – never mind the bills that came afterwards!

Jayne, 34, was no different when she was in her early 20s. She recalls, "I was a diploma holder fresh out of polytechnic, with no clue about what I wanted in my life or career. I splurged on all sorts of things and basically lived from paycheck to paycheck." She was in Taiwan at that time, working with a Singapore IT company as a project management executive and earning just enough to subsist on.

After five years of this hand-to-mouth existence in Taiwan, she came back to Singapore and took a long hard look at herself: a 25-year-old woman with not a single cent saved or asset to her name, stuck in a job that offered few prospects. Some young women may have accepted this situation as the norm and turned their energy to finding a life partner to provide financial and emotional security. Jayne, however, was disturbed by the thought that she would never be in control of her life.

"I remember saying to myself: I'm 25 and I still have nothing. What exactly do I want in life? I don't want to end up 10 years down the road with no savings, no assets and having to support my parents as an only child. My income needs to grow otherwise I'd be nowhere at the end of day; I would just be another mediocre person, and I hate to be mediocre!" Jayne recalls.

Her fears of having no money and assets was partly due to her early memories watching her father splurge, borrow and gamble until their family home had to be sold off to pay his debts. From the age of 18, Jayne and her parents lived in a series of rented apartments. "I didn't like the feeling that we couldn't have a place to call our own," she recalls.

Ten years on from that wake-up call, Jayne has far surpassed her family's and friends' expectations. Calling herself a "technologist," Jayne has carved out a niche for herself in the world of high finance, becoming one of very few women to enter the male-dominated world of project management, where her team delivers IT systems and solutions for the banking and financial industry.

Within a span of 14 years, she has applied her project management expertise in a variety of industries from banking and finance to media and telecommunications. Her income has also grown tenfold and her career has taken her to more destinations and given her more career exposure and opportunities as compared to all her friends.

"I knew that I couldn't get rich by investing in the stock market because I have no interest in following stocks. I had to focus on what I'm good at, which is my work, and I had to commit to a financial plan that gave me the outcomes I want," says Jayne. She used her steadily increasing CPF Ordinary Account savings to purchase her family home with her parents – a modest HDB five-room flat. She set herself the goal of paying off her housing loan in 10 years and met her target recently. Her car loan is also settled, making her debt-free and in an enviable position to spend or invest her money in whatever way she wants.

Now married and mother of a young son, Jayne travels Business Class, enjoys dining out with her family and friends in nice restaurants, pampers herself on spa holidays and owns a few designer handbags. She and her husband, however, were very clear about how their money should be spent on big-ticket items, even before they got married five years ago.

"When we decided to get married, we did our sums and looked at our budgets. There was a lot of pressure from both our families to stage a grand fairytale wedding at a top hotel but we both agreed that every ridiculous demand from our family members would be managed according to how we want our wedding to be," Jayne recalls.

She and her husband, who is also a project manager, managed every detail of their wedding, which was eventually held in a small, intimate hotel, attended by their closest friends, family members and relatives. "Weddings can be expensive and we said to ourselves, 'Is it worth having a fairytale wedding followed by bills and stress in our married life? Let's be realistic instead, and have something sweet and memorable' – and we did," says Jayne.

Forgoing their honeymoon, she and her husband decided to buy a car. Says Jayne, "I believe in delaying gratification – why spend unnecessarily, when you know that there are more important priorities and considerations?"

Her refusal to be financially stressed informs all her decisions about money. Jayne enrolled her son in a private kindergarten that comes with a four-figure school fee every month because she believes in giving him the best education that she can afford. Unlike many young professionals, however, she refuses to "upgrade" from her HDB flat to fancier private property, or to buy a second home. She and her husband still live happily with her parents in the flat that she bought years ago. They have no domestic help and take turns caring for their son.

"I really don't need the kind of validation that living in a District 9 or 10 brings. Nothing is really worth paying more than $1,000 per square foot for and seeing half of your paycheck going towards housing. I prefer to have my money work for me, instead of the other way round," says Jayne.

Taking the road less travelled instead of following the crowd has given Jayne the freedom to expand her horizons in other areas. She and her husband will be taking a big leap in their careers as they will be posted by their respective companies to work in the United States. She is looking forward to the move with much anticipation and excitement. "It's not about the pay but about the tremendous learning opportunity for both my husband and myself, and for our son," explains Jayne.

For a diploma holder who has worked her way up from nothing to the top of her game at age 34, Jayne has a down-to-earth philosophy about herself and her relationship with money: "Be realistic and don't set ridiculous financial goals. I've always been very clear about what I want and what to do next. Everything I do is something that I can sustain," she declares.

If money is a monster that often drives us to spend and invest recklessly, piling on debt after debt, Jayne has indeed tamed it by focusing on what's really important and meaningful to her: professional and personal growth, the happiness of her family, and most importantly, no financial stress!

FINANCIAL LIFE LESSONS

Author Oliver James coined the term "Affluenza" to describe a very insidious condition that affects all of us living in a world that's bombarded with images of successful men and women enjoying the high life – luxury cars, vacations, entertainment and residences.

According to James, "The Affluenza Virus is a set of values which increase our vulnerability to emotional distress. It entails placing a high value on acquiring money and possessions, looking good in the eyes of others and wanting to be famous."

Jayne almost succumbed to this virus too, but perhaps it was her early experiences of watching her father fall into debt thereby jeopardising the financial security of the family that galvanised her into choosing a different path. Jayne's story is compelling because she refused to be sucked into the cycle of spending and debt that so many women are prone to, simply by following a few rules:

1. Know yourself

When it comes to wealth-building, knowing what you don't want is as important as knowing what you want. Right off the bat, Jayne knew she didn't want to become a gambler like her father. As a 25-year-old, she knew that she needed to build a financial structure for her family – a structure that wouldn't crumble in the face of life's storms. Her solution was to focus on her career and be the best she can be in her chosen profession.

Building wealth by being the best at what you do is an obvious answer, yet so many of us prefer to look outside of ourselves and think that the road to wealth is guaranteed if we can learn how to trade stocks, forex and options; flip properties; or invest in exotic instruments that promise stupendous returns. Some of these so-called alternative investments, such as investing in faraway properties, ostrich farms and oil wells, have turned out to be scams.

I'm not advocating that you avoid investing in stocks or the like. Great fortunes have been built by ordinary people through timely investments in the stock and property markets. However, more often than not, great fortunes have also been lost by taking the wrong bets on the market.

Why? The fact is, not everyone has the gift, the knack for numbers, and the ability to stay cool when markets tank, as billionaire investors like Warren Buffett and Singapore's very own Peter Lim do.

We can certainly learn their techniques from the many free and useful courses provided by the Singapore Stock Exchange, Securities Investors Association (Singapore), and numerous resources on the Internet.

However, don't kid yourself into imagining that investments *alone* will provide a fast track to wealth. Don't be seduced by smooth-talking salesmen into thinking that you, too, can instantly learn to invest like Warren Buffett or be the next property millionaire – simply by attending their high-priced seminars. Even Buffett himself has made the wrong investment bets but the difference is, his pockets are deeper than yours. Which brings us to the next important point:

2. Know your risk appetite

How much are you prepared to lose if your investments don't work out? For Jayne, her answer is zero – and she isn't ashamed to say so. She isn't embarrassed to declare that she prefers to save her money the old-fashioned way – through regular savings plans.

Unlike Jayne, some of us hate to admit that we don't like or understand risky investments for fear of appearing stupid and ignorant. Especially if the person urging you to invest is a slickly dressed banker, real estate agent or financial adviser sporting an expensive watch and an expectant attitude!

The rule of thumb is to never put money in any investment that you don't understand. Question your banker and adviser, and be smart enough to listen to your gut instinct telling you if a proposal sounds too good to be true. It doesn't mean that you avoid risks altogether. Financial market risk – the risk of earning negative returns on your principal – is present in all financial products. Even your bank savings can be at risk if the bank shuts down or if interest rates fall to zero or negative!

Give yourself an acceptable range of risks and returns. Work out the maximum percent of losses you can accept and the minimum amount of returns you are prepared to earn. Using this as your guide, you can then decide on which investments work best for you and which don't.

3. Delay gratification

Jayne refused to be swept up by the Cinderella fantasy of a grand fairytale wedding in an expensive venue. The media, and sometimes even your parents, want you to believe that your wedding is a once-in-a-lifetime event, and that you should spare no expense to make it the most memorable day of your life. A wedding is indeed special, but does it have to cost you and your spouse the moon and the stars?

Many weddings have a grand start, only to see the couple end up in the divorce court years and sometimes months down the road. Do we really want to throw so much money at the beginning of the toughest and most challenging relationship of our lives? Is a big wedding the precursor to a happily-ever-after future?

"But," you may argue, "my parents want us to have a grand wedding and they are willing to pay for it!" Exactly. Weddings have become big events as a way of parents showing off rather than expressing the joy and intimacy of a union between a couple. Jayne's example shows that she and her husband were very clear about what they wanted in a wedding – a small and cosy affair that would not put them in debt as newlyweds (even if they can recoup the costs from their guests giving them money in the form of "*hong baos*"!).

They demonstrated partnership and openness in the way they discussed and handled their finances as a couple and agreed on priorities – a car instead of a honeymoon, and living in an HDB rather than private property.

4. Debt management

The "good life" is visible everywhere we go: That stunning condominium designed by an award-winning architect; the latest fine dining restaurant that everyone's talking about; that snazzy sports car and designer watch; sunning on a beach while sipping champagne.

The problem is, most of us refuse to acknowledge the hangover we get when the bills arrive. The stunning condo and snazzy sports car come with a price: years of interest payments that will keep you enslaved to the rat race – working hard not because you want to, but because you have to – to pay off those loans!

What is the opportunity cost of living beyond your means and buying something you can't afford? Instead of envisioning images of the "good life," ask yourself what's really important to you. You'll be surprised to learn that true fulfillment doesn't always come in glittering packages.

Jayne and her husband are willing to live modestly and give their son a private school education while enjoying a life of travel and adventure. Those are their values – what are yours?

Are you in debt because you wish to be respected, admired and envied by your friends and family? If you are, then you have a serious case of the Affluenza virus and your chances of achieving financial freedom are slim. It's time to refocus and tame that monster.

SUCCESS IS THE BEST MEDICINE

"**M**y business started when I discovered a great desire within me to help people achieve good health," Lisa Ng, tells me, as we sip our tea in a café filled with an office lunch crowd. Just a few weeks ago, I had seen Lisa on stage, looking every inch a queen in her elegant ball gown, as she was crowned Classic Mrs Singapore Planet 2015. Proudly walking down the red carpet by her side was her husband, Ivan. Lisa went on to the international platform to be crowned Ms Elite United Nation International 2015.

Even in that crowded café she exuded an air of glamour and confidence. In her early 50s but looking not a day older than 35, Lisa started her company, from scratch, with nothing more than her intense belief that one must always keep moving forward in life. She has since established her niche in the health and wellness sector, with a global business network of partners and customers generating a continuous flow of sales and income.

Talking to Lisa, it's hard to imagine that her journey to success started humbly. "My first marriage had ended and I had custody of my two children and received some maintenance, but not much else. I did not fight for my fair share of our assets because I was afraid that I would lose the children," she says.

They were living the high life in Shanghai where her husband was the chief financial officer of a major company. The couple were college sweethearts and after graduation, both pursued careers in banking.

Lisa herself was a corporate high flyer until her husband was posted overseas and she became a trailing spouse and expat wife. She gave up her career to take care of the children. "As a mother, I was more than willing to make this sacrifice and be 100% there for our children. I was very trusting and gave him full control of our finances. On hindsight, I should have paid more attention and maintained my own money. The irony was, I didn't expect my marriage to fail," says Lisa.

After her divorce, she moved with her children to a modest house in the suburbs of Melbourne. Those were her darkest moments as she battled sadness, anxiety and a sense of guilt that she could not provide her children with the lifestyle that they had grown accustomed to. "We had the most incredible, luxurious lifestyle – the kids were driven everywhere by the chauffeur and we had maids taking care of all our daily needs. I felt that I was depriving them of all that. We had to live on a tighter budget and I took care of all necessities. It was a far cry from what they used to enjoy," recalls Lisa.

She tried looking for work but came up with nothing. "I had left the workforce for over 10 years and it was too challenging for me to go back to my former roots in corporate banking. Not only was my knowledge outdated, I had relocated twice and couldn't apply my former work experience to the current context." She also didn't want a job that would leave her with no time for her children.

"All I could do was pray and ask God for a breakthrough," Lisa confides. With a strong faith that things would somehow work out, she decided to embark on a home-based business in network marketing with Usana, a leading US brand of nutritional health supplements. "I needed to be there for my kids and the best option in my mind was to be an entrepreneur and work on my own terms so that I wouldn't be distracted by other people's agendas and constraints," she explains. She soon found that building a customer network for her business wasn't easy. "I was in the worst possible circumstances to start a business. I had no network to speak of because I didn't know anyone after relocating twice, and I had lost touch with all my friends. All I had was trust in God's providence and my strong belief that failure was not an option!" says Lisa.

Her breakthrough in business came quietly and unexpectedly through her gardener, whom she had engaged to do some yard work. While talking to him, she found out that his wife suffered from a serious chronic skin condition. Lisa met her and introduced a nutrition programme, which eventually cleared the problem. The woman was so delighted that she not only became a regular customer but also referred Lisa to her friends.

Lisa had unlocked the secret to becoming an entrepreneur: It's not a question of asking 'how', but having the passion to ask 'why' that drives any business. "I realised that when you become focused on wanting to help people, doors will open because there are always people that you can reach out to, with needs that you can help them meet. Once you start helping them, it will basically snowball into a referral network," she shares.

One significant person she helped was a man who was suffering from chronic fatigue syndrome. Lisa poured her energy into designing a health and nutrition programme for him. Like her, he was also a survivor of a failed marriage. Their friendship blossomed into love. Today, she and Ivan are happily married and living in Singapore.

Still, it took two years of hard work for Lisa to establish herself. She faced lots of naysayers who told her that network marketing never works. "People speak from their own negative experiences but I had done my homework on Usana and found that their shares had quadrupled and they have a solid business model. I was confident that they would be a strong business partner," she says.

Her business took off and, by a mysterious law of attraction, job offers came through as well. Going back to the corporate world with its perks and titles was tempting but Lisa chose to turn them down. "I said to myself, 'No, I'm not going to take the easy way out. I'm going to be massively successful and even overtake my ex, which I've done!" Lisa exclaims.

She has reached the top tier of high achievers in Usana and enjoys passive income from her network partners in the USA, Australia, Singapore, Malaysia and the Philippines – an income that's far beyond her wildest dreams. Having achieved her goals of creating a dream life for her children, Lisa now wants to inspire and empower other women to pursue their dreams.

"Women must always dream bigger than themselves and be ready to learn new skills, especially if they have left their professional lives behind. They must stay connected to the business world with part-time work and educate themselves to keep up with what's going on. I'm a strong proponent of entrepreneurship because it's the best way for women to enlarge their finances. It also forces us to shift our mindsets and commit to personal growth and development.

"I view network marketing as a tremendous platform for women with no business experience. You pick up business skills because there's lots of support for you to learn from successful mentors. You can leverage on their experiences and the power of teamwork, without all the costs and expenses of setting up a traditional business. The networking model allows you to expand globally, too, with few overheads as compared to traditional businesses," explains Lisa.

She credits adversity as her teacher and her strong faith in God as her strength. "My divorce was a big blow to my self-confidence. I learnt that change is the norm in one's life; I had to make the hard choices that put me on the road less travelled and I had to take massive action to pursue my dream."

Lisa smiles as she reflects on her journey: "Sometimes, the winning horse wins by just a small length so I was prepared to do whatever it takes to win!" It may sound like a cliché, but for anyone who has survived a broken marriage, Lisa's story illustrates an unavoidable fact – success is the best medicine!

FINANCIAL LIFE LESSONS

No matter who's right or wrong, divorce is always a nasty and traumatic event for the family – more so when your children are young and when there's custody and financial battles brewing between you and your spouse. Divorce can even lead to tragedy. As I'm writing this, I remember a shocking incident that happened a week ago, when a loving father in Singapore strangled his 5-year-old son because he was insanely revengeful and angry with his ex-wife over custody of the boy.

Lisa was dealt a serious blow when her marriage ended. Like Andrea in an earlier chapter of this book, her comfortable life was shattered when she found out that she had very little money and needed to start life all over again. She placed her children above everything else and chose not to fight her ex-husband for her share of the marital assets. Lisa's response to her divorce illustrates some important truths:

1. Divorce is not the End but the Beginning

Sometimes, it is better to yield and accept that a broken relationship can never be repaired, rather than remain in a state of constant tension. Avoid investing all your emotional energy to right a wrong, or taking revenge by *not* granting the offending party what he or she wants – especially if your spouse is somebody wealthy and important.

Lisa's custody and financial battles with her ex could have dragged on for years, drawing her into a vortex of grief and bitterness. "Hell hath no fury like a man or woman scorned," describes the depths that we can sink to, if we allow our emotions to cloud our minds. Our scars and, more importantly, our children's scars, may never heal and the consequences can be devastating.

Although it was certainly traumatic for Lisa to let go of the luxurious life she knew, divorce may have been the best thing that happened to her. She probably wouldn't have become an entrepreneur and found her true love otherwise!

2. Adversity leads to growth

Lisa treated her divorce as a major transition in her life that caused her to "take massive action." Adversities are like 'lifequakes'; they are brilliant at shaking us. It is the Universe's signal that we are about to face new challenges, climb new mountains, and reach a higher destiny than we've ever dreamed of. Lisa could have remained a pampered wife all her life. She could have joined the bandwagon of becoming yet another corporate fixture. Instead, to quote the poet Robert Frost, she chose the road "less travelled by, and that has made all the difference." Do not be afraid of adversity. It could be your ticket to the stars.

3. Have a spiritual perspective

Sure, you may be very angry with the one who has messed up your life, but channel that anger into energy. Use that energy in prayer to connect with your divine wisdom and purpose. Lisa was sustained by her unshakeable faith in God and her belief that her painful experience is but one small blip in the universe of life. Talking to trusted friends, a coach or therapist will also give you that wider perspective. Our problems aren't unique and there's always a way out of the tunnel. Others have clawed their way out, so why not you? Look for the rainbow after the rain.

4. Have a vision and stick to it

While counselling my clients, I often ask them to imagine what they would like their life to look like if a miracle were to happen. I'm not encouraging wishful thinking but rather, a deep, personal visualisation about a positive outcome in your life. Imagine how you would feel if your problems are resolved. What will you be doing? How will your children and close friends describe you? Lisa's vision was simple: She was going to show her former husband that she didn't need him. She was going to be that winning horse, winning on her own terms. Guided by her vision, her "miracle" came true!

5. Be your own person

Sadly, it usually takes a lifequake like divorce and widowhood for women to wake up and realise that they are financially vulnerable. We tend to embrace our traditional roles of being wives and mothers at the expense of our own personal development and financial health.

Bright, intelligent women like Lisa who marry the proverbial "Prince Charming" – top professionals, corporate honchos and men of great wealth – are often lulled into thinking that they are set for life. We can't help it – it's the conditioning that has been ingrained into our consciousness in stories like Cinderella, movies like *Pretty Woman*, and countless romance novels.

Women who are married to high-powered men also tend to take a backseat for fear that they will outshine their husbands and they're not wrong – successful men do tend to be highly egocentric. They often want their wives to be their trophies rather than equal working partners. Jacqueline Kennedy Onassis, for example, only came into her own after her two husbands had died. However, as more women claim their right to be on equal footing with men in their professional lives, we will find more marriages like that of Amal and George Clooney's – high-powered human rights lawyer married to high-powered Hollywood actor!

If you find yourself in the comfortable position of being a Mrs Somebody, avoid "retiring" yourself from the working world. From your privileged position, you can still hone your professional skills with part-time work and consulting that will keep you in the loop. You may also study for a degree, write a blog, join non-profit organisations, teach and volunteer. Develop your own professional contacts and circle of friends so that you won't be completely lost and bereft if, God forbid, your husband leaves you! Throughout your marriage, take time to build and maintain your own financial health portfolio.

6. Be your own boss

Lisa was not afraid to change course and become a network marketing entrepreneur. Women who have been out of the workforce for a while often complain that they have "missed the bus." They are too old, they have no skills, and they don't know anyone who would give them a break.

Men have the same complaints, too, as the concept of lifetime employment followed by a stable pension is fast disappearing. Retrenchment is the norm and even those in top management can find themselves out of work at a moment's notice. When the rug under your feet is suddenly pulled, is there something else that you can stand on?

Yes, there is. It's your ability to sell. No one needs an MBA to be able to sell something – be it goods in a market, cakes that you bake, real estate, insurance, or supplements. These are the areas where being sincere and having an interest in people and a desire to help them can ultimately result in huge financial rewards as Lisa has found.

Selling real estate and insurance requires you to sit for exams and be licensed. Selling products that you source or make requires an investment of your time, money and overheads such as office space and equipment. I have a friend who travels extensively to exotic locations to buy local handicrafts and decorative items to sell in Singapore boutiques. As a single woman, my friend enjoys her nomadic lifestyle. However, as a single mum, such an investment of time and money may be impossible.

Network marketing is ideal because you can start by becoming a distributor immediately, working from home from your computer. There are many kinds of products that you can distribute through network marketing. Choose a product and a network partner that you like and believe in. Lisa was interested in holistic health and nutrition and she researched and found a company that not only matched her philosophy, but also has the track record and business plan to support her growth.

7. Conquer your fear of selling

I started my sales career 14 years ago and I can honestly say that it's the best 'University of Life' that I've ever had! It brought me out of my cocoon, forced me to conquer my fear of approaching strangers, and made me a better listener. I became more emotionally resilient in the face of rejection and criticism. Sales does that to you: Salespeople who get up again and again after being knocked down develop the art of standing their ground and earning more money than they've ever dreamed of, like Lisa.

However, if you cannot stomach rejection and criticism, you would be limiting your income earning options severely. Many administrative and manufacturing jobs and even professional services such as accounting and graphic design are fast disappearing and may even vanish one day, as more companies outsource their work to cheaper workers online. In the near future, more job functions will be replaced by computers, robots and drones.

We need to reframe our perspectives and prejudices about becoming salespeople. Think about it: We sell as often as we breathe! In our daily lives, we are always listening, negotiating, pitching, convincing, persuading and speaking out. Selling skills have actually been pre-programmed in us from the beginning of time as a pre-requisite for our survival.

So, don't imagine yourself hustling products no one wants. Instead, visualise yourself becoming a valuable human resource, just as Lisa visualises herself as a holistic health educator. Imagine yourself as a people connector, a go-to expert, a big sister, a fairy godmother … in other words, weave your life experiences, your interests and your personality into your sales story.

In our big, impersonal world, drones, machines and computers cannot provide the human touch – but salespeople can. We all have the power to touch strangers and make a difference in their lives. Lisa's breakthrough came when she empathised with her gardener's wife and connected with her. The only way to learn how to sell is to just do it, as Lisa has discovered.

THE ACCIDENTAL ENTREPRENEUR

Women have always been great at multi-tasking; they wear multiple hats as wives, mothers and caregivers for the young and elderly, while holding full-time or part-time jobs or even running their own businesses.

We often don't see our ability to multi-task as anything special. After all, our prevailing cultural norm prescribes that all women are brought up with the expectation that they have to serve, to nurture and to give. It takes courage and determination for a woman to write a new script for herself – without sacrificing or forsaking her family.

My friend Veronica Tan, however, is one brave woman who has done just that. When I first met her more than 10 years ago, Veronica was a young wife and mother of three who worked at The Salvation Army. She was the sole breadwinner supporting her family of five on her monthly income of $1,900.

Fast forward to the present when I interviewed her for this book, Veronica is better known as the founder and CEO of Rev22, a company that specialises in therapeutic bedding and accessories. Full of positive energy, she is always excited and enthusiastic as she talks about how her original line of Energia pillows, mattresses, socks, eye masks and neck pillows have helped to improve insomnia and relieve her customers' pain and chronic health conditions.

Her brand is now carried in 10 retail outlets around the island and her business success is seen in the many glowing testimonials she receives from her customers and followers on her website and Facebook page.

Entrepreneurship was in her genes even before she knew it, she recalls. "I grew up in a provision (grocery) shop owned by my grandfather and father. From a very young age I was already helping my father in his shop every day after school. I had no school holidays or weekends off and I learnt how to earn money."

After she left school, she couldn't wait to escape from the drudgery of working in her family's grocery shop and applied to train as a nurse because it would give her a stable income. She says, "Becoming my own boss never crossed my mind then. It was too much hard work, I thought. I didn't want to be like my parents, selling *ikan bilis* (dried fish) for the rest of my life." Although her salary as a staff nurse back in the early 1980s was just under $500 per month, she made the most of it, enjoying herself on holiday trips abroad with her friends.

One of them introduced her to the man who was to become her husband. Ben* (not his real name) was well-educated and articulate, having just returned from the United States with a bachelor's degree in business. He walked with a limp due to childhood polio and had a job in a hardware store. He was also trying to start a small business as an employment consultant for Singapore nurses who wanted to work in the USA.

The couple had a whirlwind courtship and were soon married. "Ben came from a large family in Malaysia who were very warm, open and affectionate with one another. They represented all the values and qualities that I missed in my own family, and I suppose I was drawn to him and his family as a whole, more than Ben the person," she says. They had no money to buy a home and moved into a rented room until her first pregnancy. They managed to buy an HDB apartment during her pregnancy and shifted into the flat just before her son was born. Unlike Ben's family who warmly welcomed her as one of their own, Veronica's mother was disappointed by her choice and acted aloof towards him.

Veronica herself was beginning to question whether she had indeed made a mistake. "After our marriage, I experienced a 'culture shock'," she says. I've always been very disciplined and worked hard all my life, but there he was, sleeping late, waking up late, and lazing around. I really had to adjust my expectations," she remembers.

By this time, her husband had already abandoned his previous plan to be an employment consultant and was a struggling insurance agent. Says Veronica, "He hated approaching people and couldn't take rejection so I decided to help him with sales prospecting while taking care of my son at home. I talked to our neighbours, shop owners and anyone I knew, even our fishmonger, and asked them if they wanted to buy insurance and helped him close sales."

The devout Roman Catholic never considered giving up on her marriage. "What could I do?" she exclaims. "I talked to my priest who told me that marriage is not a bed of roses. I just had to accept my situation for what it is and live day to day."

After her eldest son was born, Veronica stopped work and advertised herself as a part-time nanny to boost the family income. She took care of another infant while still nursing her own son. By the time her second child, a daughter, was born, the couple agreed that Ben would stay home to look after the children while Veronica became the family breadwinner. She was soon hired to run The Salvation Army daycare centre for the elderly in Bedok.

"My workplace was near our home so I walked to work and saved on transport. We followed a strict budget. Lunch was provided at work and I often brought any leftover food from The Salvation Army back home for dinner," recalls Veronica.

As expenses increased, Veronica worked as a private nurse on Saturdays, earning an additional $880 a month, which she used to pay for her children's music lessons and other enrichment classes. Her private nursing stint lasted five years.

"I even joined a multi-level marketing company. The few times that I hit the company's sales target, I was rewarded with holiday trips to Bali and Malacca. Those were the only times we could travel overseas and enjoy ourselves as a family," she says, reliving her lean years.

The one bright spot in her life was her work. "The Salvation Army daycare centre became my playground. I did not see myself as an employee. As the manager of the centre, I took ownership of the place and ran it as if it was my own business," says Veronica. She initiated many national events and projects to uplift the spirits of the elderly such as an Intergenerational Sports Day, Intergenerational Harmony Day, Intergenerational *Amazing Race* and Intergenerational Beach Party, and even organised holiday trips to Malacca and Ipoh in Malaysia.

"My personal motto was, as long the old folks are spending the day with us, I'll make sure that it's a memorable day for them," she adds. She was also managing the accounts, personnel, marketing and sponsorship activities but she never questioned the salary she was receiving – her take-home pay was just $1,400. "I didn't fight for my pay for a very long time because I saw my work as a vocation," she explains.

However, the CEO of The Salvation Army's Peacehaven Nursing Home visited the daycare centre one day and was impressed with what he saw – Veronica had turned it around from a deficit into a profit centre. He promptly went about setting things right and increased her salary and yearly bonus. Says Veronica, "I'm very grateful and thankful for the 10 years that I spent at The Salvation Army. It was truly my training ground that prepared me to become an entrepreneur."

While her work was deeply satisfying, life at home was stormy. Ben was a capable househusband and caring Dad but he was prone to temper outbursts whenever he saw Veronica. Theirs was a relationship that see-sawed between love and war.

Looking back at those challenges, Veronica believes that whatever she had gone through was God-ordained, even her difficult marriage. In fact, it was Ben who inspired her to start her own business.

"Our children were growing up and doing well in school and I was overjoyed when Ben decided to embrace the Catholic faith and got baptised. I hoped he would be a changed man and peace would be restored to our home," recalls Veronica. Ben's newfound faith had indeed awakened in him and gifted him with amazing spiritual insights and healing powers. People were soon seeking him for spiritual counselling and healing. "After his baptism, he had a vision that I would be running a successful business that would help many people," adds Veronica.

Confident that they were headed for a fresh start, she resigned from The Salvation Army and invested in a line of alkaline water filters, her first product. "I had to buy 300 pieces and didn't have much money so, I asked my children to sacrifice their *hong bao* money in their piggy banks," recalls Veronica. "I soon managed to clear all my stock by operating a push cart outside a Traditional Chinese Medicine clinic in a bustling neighbourhood."

It was during this period that she met the inventor of the therapeutic mattress and bedding products. Veronica found that it healed her of her own chronic health conditions and immediately sensed that she had found a good business opportunity. She, Ben and the inventor became business partners. However, they had to weather the ups and downs of creating and sustaining sales. "We made a quarter of a million dollars in our first month in 2010 selling the inventor's products. But in 2011, we came close to losing everything!" she remembers.

She and Ben had to pick themselves up and start all over again. They persevered and imported their own brand of therapeutic sleep products, Energia (Spanish for 'energy'), in 2012. Today, the company is growing steadily and Veronica is planning to expand overseas. Keen to hone her entrepreneurial skills and learn as much as she can,

Veronica has even engaged a business coach to prepare her for the next lap.

Just like her time at The Salvation Army, Veronica infuses her business and her team of marketing support staff with enthusiasm, passion and commitment. Her sales promoters actively demonstrate the benefits of Energia products at retail outlets, roadshows and health events. Customers on her mailing list are regularly invited to attend special parties as well as talks and workshops on health topics.

While she invests heavily in the business, Veronica maintains a frugal lifestyle. She drives a goods van, which doubles as her delivery van, and she doesn't spend much on herself.

"I've always spent within my means and avoided borrowing money for personal expenses. When I do spend money, I spend on items that will help to grow the business such as a professionally designed website, brochures and marketing materials," she explains.

This caused conflicts between her and Ben who wanted to keep a tight rein on business expenses. She and Ben couldn't see eye-to-eye on so many business and personal issues that they have chosen to live apart for the last three years. They are currently trying to mend their marriage through counselling.

"Everything happens for a reason. Even when my husband left, it was a blessing. That was when I really came into my own and grew the business. When he was around, I tended to defer to him because he's the one with the bachelor's degree whereas I'm just a nurse after all!" she says.

Her advice for women? "Just do your best in whatever situation you find yourself in, good or bad. A lot of things are beyond our control and we just have to manage them as they come. Be the best mother or wife you can be and move on. Worrying about your life doesn't help because it saps your energy. I always ask myself what is the best I could achieve for the day and leave it there," she declares.

As always, the accidental entrepreneur credits her faith for bringing her to where she is today. "My satisfaction comes from seeing God's hand at work in every milestone of our company's growth. We are a team that glorifies God in our business."

FINANCIAL LIFE LESSONS

Depending on one's response, adversity can either be a great teacher or a great destroyer. Veronica did not have any big dreams or ambitions when she was a young woman. She was simply content to work as a nurse in a professional career that would provide her with a steady income for the rest of her life. A series of circumstances led her to discover her talents as an entrepreneur and made her who she is today. Veronica's story illustrates some important truths:

1. You are bigger than your mistakes and failures

We all make mistakes in our life choices such as choosing the wrong career, the wrong spouse, the wrong property, and the wrong investment. It is natural to brood over our mistakes and be miserable. As Veronica says, we must move on from our disappointments and failures. We must allow our mistakes to strengthen us rather than diminish us. Veronica did not try to change her husband or seek to escape from a marriage that was less than what she expected. She accepted her spouse's weaknesses and took a bold step to become the family breadwinner. It was her less-than-perfect marriage that eventually propelled her to become an entrepreneur.

2. Stop underselling yourself

Most women have a habit of underselling themselves, their abilities and their talents. We often look up to those with master's and bachelor degrees and look down on ourselves if we lack qualifications. It is a pity that in Singapore, our educational institutions and employers in the public and private sectors seem to place greater importance on paper qualifications than on life skills and character.

Veronica only saw herself as a lowly nurse and thought that her husband was more qualified to run a business than she was. Little did she realise that by running a daycare centre profitably, working as a private nurse, balancing the family budget, and helping her husband sell insurance, she was far more talented than she gave herself credit for, and could draw on these strengths as an entrepreneur.

Take an honest look at yourself (you may want to do this with the help of a career/life coach) and ask yourself if you have been discounting your abilities and talents. Have you been allowing others to take credit for the work you do? Do you deliberately shy away from recognition because you feel less deserving than someone who has a degree? This 'underselling' mindset can prevent you from growing professionally and financially. It's time to snap out of it.

3. Cultivate your personal oasis

Veronica's personal oasis in her difficult marriage was her faith in God and a job that allowed her to bring joy and happiness to seniors at The Salvation Army daycare centre. Cultivating your peace of mind in the midst of problems and stress could be as simple as setting aside 20 minutes a day to breathe, meditate, pray, go for a walk or relax in a hot bath. Or it could be devoting time to a hobby you enjoy. The fun Veronica had at work helped her cope with the tensions at home.

4. Separate your personal from your professional

Working with a spouse can be tricky, as tensions in the marriage can easily spill over into work and vice versa. The ability to compartmentalise is something that we can all learn. Draw clear boundaries between work and personal issues. Veronica never allowed her tensions in her marriage to affect her focus at work or distract her from pursuing her vision for her business.

5. Life is a "work-in-progress"

Veronica's story shows that we can manage whatever challenges we face in life – even if we don't have a perfect answer or solution. She has weathered lean times, taking on two to three jobs to support her family. She has survived business failure and even emptied her children's piggy banks! Her business is a work-in-progress, so is her marriage. She is doing the best she can, under her present circumstances. She is seeking help from a business coach for her business and seeing a marriage counsellor. Through the ups and downs of her journey, she has become a successful woman.

PART 4:

Leaning In with Tara Kimbrell Cole

AN INTERVIEW

We have heard the voices of several women as they recount their experiences in life, the setbacks they faced and the insights they gained as they journeyed through careers, marriage, motherhood, divorce and retirement. From the stories I've gathered, I realised that our financial well-being cannot be separated from our physical, mental, emotional and spiritual well-being.

The women who seem to "have it together" and are most satisfied with their lives are those who have found their sense of purpose and meaning in life. They are independent in every sense of the word – free to make their own decisions and free to design their own lives – not according to what society tells them, but what their hearts tell them. They are free to think out of the box and are not afraid to use their talents to contribute to the world in their own special ways. Most important of all, they are no longer slaves to money but masters of it.

Perhaps no one understands this better than Tara Kimbrell Cole, CEO of Synovations Pte Ltd. She founded the consulting firm in Singapore in 2003 to create, design and deliver organisational development programmes to build leadership, systems thinking, innovation capabilities, change management, and team collaboration across a broad range of industries. Known for championing women's causes, Tara has been a featured speaker at the UN Global Summit of Women (Davos for Women), the ASEAN Women's Summit, and The International Alliance for Women Annual Forum.

Although she counts Microsoft, BHP Billiton, Standard Chartered Bank, National University of Singapore Business School, and Singapore Management University Executive Development among her top clients, Tara is also passionate about coaching executive women to develop their full potential. One of the vehicles through which she does this is Synovations' Lean In Circles sessions.

Lean In Circles is an initiative that was inspired by the book *Lean In: Women, Work, and the Will to Lead* by Sheryl Sandberg, Chief Operating Officer of Facebook. The book, which has climbed bestseller lists to become the modern working woman's Bible, examines the progress of women in the corporate world, the reasons why so few women have achieved leadership roles, and what we can do about it. The book's popularity has led to the Lean In Circles movement, where women everywhere, from all trades, professions and businesses, have been encouraged to form Lean In Circles to drive awareness and support and encourage one another. (For more information on Lean In Circles, go to www.leanin.org/circles)

I met Tara at her home, a black and white colonial bungalow surrounded by verdant greenery. As our conversation unfolded, I discovered a woman of great intellect and wisdom, who has walked through many paths in life to become her own person. She doesn't mince words when it comes to sharing her views about women and money, and how women can define themselves in the modern world. The following is the interview I conducted with her:

Tara, as CEO of Synovations, you have really achieved a lot on your own terms. How did you start out?

I worked in financial services in New York and then started my own boutique merchant banking company specialising in the financing of letters of credit and bank guarantees. I was not trained in finance; I had graduated with a fine arts degree. In the 1980s, that wasn't so unusual – there were many women who were getting into business, who were trained on the job, learning from the rough and tumble of experience. You kept learning as the work and role required. I had an innate understanding of business, finance and entrepreneurship, and remained in finance for over 20 years.

What brought you to this part of the world?

My partner died unexpectedly and then the US tax laws, which fuelled that business sector changed – both within a year of each other. I was at a particularly sensitive point in my life where these unexpected changes presented a huge challenge. I asked myself at the time: "If I were to see my glass as half-full rather than empty, what action would I take? What would inspire me?" My answer was to take a sabbatical to see the parts of the world I knew little about. I had travelled in the industrialised world but I knew nothing of the lesser-developed world. I wanted to understand the other world and the Southern Hemisphere, so I spent a year in Africa and four years travelling in the Asia Pacific.

During my sabbatical, I studied psychology, Asian cultures, and philosophy. Five years later, I had a very different perspective of the world. When I went back to work, my "knee-jerk" reaction was to go back into finance. Exploring for opportunities, I discovered that there was a need for a specialised form of export finance (forfaiting) in Asia that had, until then, only existed for developed countries' exporters trading with emerging markets but not for emerging market exporters. I founded a company to serve as the exclusive Asia representative of BB Aval GmbH Germany (BBA), a trade finance (forfaiting) subsidiary of Berliner Bank AG. After the Asian financial crisis of 1997, I remained in Asia and founded Global Trade Finance Network™ Pte Ltd (GTFNet), a software company.

Around 2002, I decided that it was time to apply much of what I had learned during my sabbatical years. I obtained training in organisational learning, leadership development, and executive coaching. Historically, psychology was applied to treat people who were sick, but in the 1980s and 1990s, the business schools began applying self-awareness and human development concepts to the advancement of executives and leaders. I wanted to join in this development and most particularly in the work of Massachusetts Institute of Technology (MIT) and the Society for Organizational Learning.

Going to Africa, starting a business in Asia, switching from finance to coaching – that's a lot of changes! How easy was it for you to make these transitions?

It didn't come about without a certain amount of pain pushing me to make a change. If not for the dramatic events that affected my business and personal life and the timing of them, I may not have even looked at making the changes because I would have seen the world as I always had. That was a perspective that sees New York as the centre of the world! Why would anyone want to go anywhere else?

I had been raised to have a very traditional life. Suddenly, I found myself completely on my own, at an age when I wanted to have children. It was pretty shocking for me – my business was changing and I was feeling burnt out. Change was a big hurdle. I took some self-awareness seminars, worked with a spiritual teacher and decided to explore newly discovered interests, including things that inspired me – in contrast to that which I was taught to be interested in.

What were the pressures you faced growing up?

In my family, you either became a doctor or a lawyer. Going to business school was not part of the conversation or on the list of options. In those days, young women weren't going to business school. I studied fine arts because I felt that was what I was interested in, but it did not prepare me to make a living. Life doesn't happen the way you plan it. I had to unravel a lot of old ideas – it really is first, a revolution in one's head and an individual journey. Carl Jung called the journey "individuation."

Can you elaborate on what you went through in this process of unravelling, and how women can have "a revolution in their heads" as you put it?

It's good to get as much guidance as you can. Today there are life coaches such as myself who work with women. In the old days, there were only therapists. They serve very different functions. I have always been passionate about the teachings of Carl Jung. As far back as the 1930s, he wrote about his theory on a way for women to deal with their "animus" (an inner masculine part of the female personality, often a critic). Jung proposed building one's own self-worth and confidence from doing what you love to do as an effective way to deal with the negative critic in your head.

I did a lot of work on myself psychologically and spiritually. I was developing my own philosophical perspective and preparing myself to live as a contemporary woman in a contemporary world, in contrast to the world I had known as a child. I realised that in every woman's journey, there are always decisions that she has made that bring her to where she is, but the key is in how one takes that forward from the current reality. No one can fix the past; one can only accept it.

You had a certain amount of financial independence that enabled you to make these changes and redesign your life. What are your views about financial independence?

I think there are multiple aspects to financial independence. One is figuring out the work that you can do that supports you, no matter what happens to your investments. One can save and be prudent in preparing for the future, but not to the point where you are consumed with worry about the future that you're never enjoying the present. This sounds so obvious but life is meant to be lived. We never know how long we're going to live! Spending all your time not living today so that you're saving for tomorrow is a very sad way to waste your life.

I don't believe in "retirement" in the conventional sense. The time to change your life usually happens in your 40s, plus or minus. Something will happen to you around that time that will put you at a crossroads. In my case, I took a significant break from work to re-evaluate my life and decide what to do next. I have always thought it would be a terrible feeling to be older and irrelevant. I had noticed that the older people who were enjoying life were active, engaged and contributing back, not sitting around – how boring would that be! We all have much longer lives to live than we perceived when we were younger.

Older women in Singapore who have to restart their lives all over again often face a lot of closed doors. What's your advice?

It's cruel anywhere in the world for older women, because we have societies focused on younger women. So this exacerbates the issue. Even though you may feel burnt out at that mid-point, the odds today are that you still have another 40 years to go. And you're likely to have to do it on your own! You may be in a good marriage or you may not. But this is the time for women to discover and build on their own interests, rather than sitting around and following their husbands, partners and/or children.

Besides the issue of ageing, what are the obstacles that women generally face if they want to grow?

When I started my business in Asia in the early 1990s, people found it strange that my company was representing a bank in Europe – it just didn't fit their picture because they hadn't seen it before. It was the same with entrepreneurship. Singapore has totally changed its perspective on that and that shift took about 20 years. There is a lot of discouragement out there. Sometimes, women are discouraged by the very men they admire or trust. I'm confident that if all the capable women in the world were to come forward, they'd be taking jobs away from some of the men. That's part of the issue. And we need more capable women to come forward. The world run by men has been – and is – imbalanced, and not a world that most people feel positive about.

Young girls are still not taught that they will need to take care of themselves one day. To do so, they will need to learn about managing their own finances. Little girls are taught to behave and be "good girls" so that some man will come along and "take care of you"! It's acceptable for a boy to head a technology company but little girls are not taught that they could be just as capable of doing so. That's a major point of Sheryl Sandberg's Lean In initiative. It asks us to challenge these unconscious stereotypes and assumptions.

This inhibition about money and fear that we don't know how to manage ourselves and take care of ourselves starts when we're very young. Is that the natural mindset or the programming? I see women independent contractors allow their clients to pay them late. If a male independent contractor is not paid in three months, he'll be at the company door to collect! I think women get their emotions mixed up with money because they unconsciously think it's about being a good little girl. The contracting company becomes "Daddy."

So, what's the solution?

We women need to understand our own mental models: Clarify for ourselves what really matters to each of us and master the ability to achieve it. Understand what mindset is your own and what has been appropriated from your family and culture. We need to identify and silence our own respective internal critics; the voices that undermine us with negative messages that drive self-doubt and fear.

For example, if you get a headache every time you think about your finances, you need to understand what's happening and work through it, learn about it. Running away or having someone else take care of it won't help either. We women often undermine ourselves by not learning about what we need to do to take care of ourselves. Many women become victims of bad financial advice because we don't know how to evaluate what the financial adviser is doing.

However, there are many women who start out in life looking after their husbands and children, and they never had the education or advantages that you had ...

I believe that managing the home and children is enormous preparation for dealing with a business. Women are obliged to multitask and address multiple challenges at once, moving fluidly from one to the next. Women have the natural ability to take what they learn in the kitchen and apply it outside. I believe confidence in women should be running high and yet, it's a lack of confidence that undermines most women.

Education is essential. Investing in one's education at every stage of life is critical today. That is the most important investment one can make. If you're not in a position to invest in a degree, you can still keep learning. The Internet offers access to the world's libraries and schools. MIT, Harvard and many other top universities around the world offer free courses online.

It's the lack of self-confidence fuelled by the internal critic that inhibits many women from going out and learning what they need to learn. Learning how to calibrate self-talk with supportive messages can help. We all have voices in our heads. Learning how to deal with those voices and develop personal mastery with one's self can give us the support and courage to deal with challenges. Otherwise, whatever you do can be easily sabotaged by fear and a lack of confidence.

Were you ever fearful? What have you learnt from your fears?

Yes. The greatest mistakes I've ever made were made from fear. I've lost money from investments because I've invested from a defensive fearful position and changed my investment decisions out of fear instead of holding firm. In contrast, the best decisions I've ever made, were made out of a full understanding of the possibilities and consequences of my choice while listening to my intuition. Those decisions turned out to be good ones. Whenever I was coming from the fearmonger – telling me that I must do this or that to defend against the fear – it resulted in negative outcomes.

With the financial markets being so volatile, making the right decisions can be difficult.

I agree, and to make things worse, there are lots of people out there selling all sorts of junk and junky ideas. Following the crowd will usually get one into trouble.

So, what's the best way for a woman to achieve financial freedom? Entrepreneurship?

There's no one simple answer and entrepreneurship is not by any means right for everyone. Before you jump into anything, get to know who you are, what inspires you, what your capabilities are realistically, and explore how you might apply them. Ask yourself how you could serve. Choose to do something you love because you'll be doing a lot of it. One can't control the bigger system nor stop a financial market from imploding. You could have investments that you thought were perfect, and still lose money from the volatility in the markets! However, what we won't ever lose is our own learning, our own selves, our experience, and hopefully our desire to survive. I like the concept that Deepak Chopra proposed in that one finds one's security in uncertainty.

How can a woman benefit from Lean In Circles?

Seminal research about women is presented from which women can understand themselves better as well as that of our collective predicament. Lean In enables one to align with other women to bring the changes forward. Self-awareness is an important key in resolving our issues: Understand the collective biases and problems in the system outside oneself; learn about the challenges women share and the challenges that you as an individual can overcome by shifting your own mindset; and welcome change and the willingness to do things differently.

What's your final message for women?

Women have so much value to bring to the world. I don't know anyone who thinks the world is going on very well right now, and yet there's a complete imbalance – our voices are not heard equally to our demographic footprint. We are 51 percent of the population! There's huge opportunity for women to realise their strengths and contribute to a better life for all.

PART 5:
Next Steps

LET'S IMPROVE
OUR FINANCIAL FITNESS

As I write this concluding section of this book, I realise that are still more experiences for women to share and more stories to be told – if only more will come forward and share them openly without shame.

Tara Kimbrell Cole was right when she shared in the previous chapter that women need to go through "a revolution in our heads" before we can begin to discard the wrong beliefs and behaviour patterns that we have grown up with, such as the belief that managing one's money is a chore and a necessary evil, like taking bitter medicine. Or the belief that if a woman is blessed with a good husband and strong marriage, the money will take care of itself.

There's also this happy-go-lucky voice in our heads that tells us that it's far better to enjoy life without worrying about bills, saving for retirement, or writing a will because hey, we'll cross the bridge when we get to it. If a well-educated professional like my Dad can be an ostrich when it comes to money, what about the rest of us? Trust me, our financial problems and inability to handle our money are not unique but we'd be the last to admit it because money issues are often cloaked in secrecy and denial.

No one dared to pull my Dad aside, get him to look at his balance sheet, encourage him to talk honestly about his money management, and work out an action plan to rebuild his life step-by-step. It was just too painful for him to confront his money issues. He suffered in silence until the stress killed him. He's not the only one. Money problems have always ranked as one of the leading causes of depression and suicide worldwide.

Ironically, the only way to enjoy a happy-go-lucky existence is to take care of our money: not just once a year, not when we feel like it, but consistently. Does this suggestion make you a little uncomfortable? (I can already imagine some of you rolling your eyes!) Yes, we all want to be millionaires but hate to be "bean counters," don't we?

It's time to change your mindset and get rid of the emotional baggage, stereotypes, guilt, envy, denial and fantasies associated with money. Your relationship with your money is nothing more than a business relationship. You are the mistress and your money merely follows your guidance, leadership and control. It should never have the power to give you sleepless nights, fear or worry.

And the way to take care of your financial health is no different from taking care of your physical health. Here's how I would equate taking care of yourself both physically and financially:

Physical Health	Financial Health
Brush and floss your teeth twice a day and see your dentist every 6 months.	Track your spending – money in and money out. Work out a monthly and annual spending plan.
Avoid over-consuming sugary and high calorie drinks and food, as this will lead to obesity and life threatening diseases.	Control your credit card usage and pay off your bills in full. If not, this will balloon into more debt with high interest rates.
Eat a balanced diet comprised of healthy, non-processed foods. Beware of foods that come with labels you don't understand.	Practice asset allocation and avoid exotic investments that you don't understand.

Exercise with cardio-vascular workouts (e.g. brisk walking, jogging and dancing) and strength-building exercises.	Put cash aside to create your Emergency Fund, Periodic Expenses Fund as well as your Freedom Fund.
Schedule a yearly medical check-up to keep track of your health.	Review your financial goals once a year and adjust where necessary.

Except for the super fit, very few of us would be able to tick "Yes" on all the boxes under physical health, let alone financial health! I want you to know that it's okay. None of us are angels when it comes to food, exercise or money. My purpose in creating this table is not to illustrate what a weak person you are but to give you a mental model and awareness of how we can manage our money consistently and unemotionally.

If we can start to apply just one habit from the list above, all the rest will follow naturally and we will see amazing results. For example, if you choose to exercise regularly, you will feel better and look better. It would cause you to watch what you eat and make healthy habits a part of your life. Likewise, by practicing one good money habit regularly, such as using a debit card instead of a credit card, you will free yourself from becoming a debt slave and improve your financial health significantly.

THE DANGERS OF 'MONEY FOG'

However, applying good money habits is easier said than done. We are surrounded by temptations calling out to us constantly, leading us to spend our money impulsively on "non-essentials." *The Sunday Times,* Singapore's national newspaper, reported in a recent survey commissioned by VISA credit card that women in Singapore spent on average 46% of their weekly personal expenses (roughly equivalent to $51.76 per week) on unplanned purchases such as buying snacks, leisure shopping and coffee breaks. (*The Sunday Times,* December 13, 2015)

This works out to more than $2,000 per year – money that could be set aside in a regular investment or savings plan. At very conservative returns of 5% per year, you would be $26,413 richer in 10 years.

Yes, we err because we're human. I confess I've given in to the urge to spend more than I earn – simply because I've had a bad day at work! The emotions driving us to gamble and overspend are the same emotions that drive us to overeat rich, calorie-laden foods, ice cream, cakes and desserts, and drink too many $7 lattes. We want to numb our pain and boredom. Shit happens and life gets us down. The easiest way to deal with our disappointments is finding comfort in the primal ritual of putting food in our mouths as well as buying more stuff.

When we get into this state of "money fog," it keeps us from looking at the Big Picture of Life and achieving what we truly want. Is it really financially impossible for you to buy a nicer home, travel around the world or go back to school for that master's degree? Or have you fallen into a mode of silent resignation, running on a hamster wheel to pay your bills while incurring more debt? Are you pushing aside your dreams and living on autopilot?

As a former financial adviser, I've often met women who do not want to commit to a regular review of their finances because they fear that I would advise them to put more money aside for savings, investments or insurance.

Putting money aside regularly to address the larger goals in one's life is akin to having a root canal. There's pain, discomfort and sacrifice in the short term. It's not much fun because you feel a sense of deprivation (less money to spend on lattes). There's anxiety, too – that the promised returns from the financial product would be disappointing. It's far easier not to think about money, carrying on as we always have, and longing for something better but not knowing what to do about it.

It doesn't have to be this way. We don't need to feel deprived or out of control. We can put ourselves at the steering wheel of our financial health – steering ourselves away from trouble and towards the life that we are meant to live.

A WORD ABOUT FINANCIAL FREEDOM

But how does one get from 0 to 10 on the money fitness scale? Many wealth gurus will tell you that the ultimate goal is to aim for financial freedom. This is the ideal situation where you'll have passive income flowing in from several assets.

According to Robert Kiyosaki (author of *Rich Dad, Poor Dad*), anyone can be a "Rich Dad" if you learn to master the property game, the business game, the forex game … the list goes on and on. If you learn the secrets of the super rich, you'll never have to work again, and live happily ever after!

That's only half the story because passive income demands active work – plus luck and timing. I'll draw another fitness analogy – one that all women can identify with. Do you sometimes wish that you can look amazing, with not a kilo of extra fat or cellulite, like those Hollywood actresses or supermodels? Well, have you thought about how many hours of working out and how many personal trainers, chefs, hairstylists, makeup artists and plastic surgeons they hire, for them to look stunning?

In the same way, very few of us can achieve the self-made wealth of a Richard Branson or Steve Jobs. Unless you have the time, passion or interest to follow the latest developments of the financial markets daily, plus the discipline to take massive action and risk occasional losses, trying to be a "Rich Dad" will only frustrate, and may even bankrupt, you.

There's also another reality check: According to the 2015 wealth report by Credit Suisse, almost half of global wealth (45%) is owned by just 0.7% of the world's richest people. Where does Singapore fit into this? Five percent of Singaporeans are in the top 1% of global wealth holders. To reach the ranks of the super rich isn't easy – despite the best efforts of wealth gurus who tell us that we can beat the odds.

So the rest of us in the 95% will have to adjust our expectations and ask ourselves honestly, what is our own definition of wealth and financial freedom? (Never mind what the wealth gurus say). How can we engage our money in a way that answers our physical, emotional, mental and spiritual needs, and gives us total peace of mind? How can we reach a state of contentment and feel wealthy where we're at – knowing exactly how our money should serve us?

MONEY FITNESS COACHING

Having experienced the consequences of money fog (mine and my father's), I realised that I want to be an agent of change rather than an agent of financial products and services. I decided that my mission would be to help women, especially, to get over the years of cultural conditioning and self-defeating behaviours that are preventing them from becoming the masters of their money.

I started moneyfitcoach.com to bridge the gap between traditional credit counselling, psychotherapy, life coaching, and financial planning. This new discipline, called 'Financial Therapy' has been gaining ground in the last three years. According to an August 19, 2013 report on USnews.com on "The Benefits of Financial Therapy":

"Anyone who's argued with a spouse over credit card bills or wrestled with their own spending habits knows that money and emotions are often inextricably linked. Yet until recently, most therapists focused on the emotional side of the equation without talking numbers, while financial planners stuck to retirement plans or investment strategies without considering their client's preconceptions or emotions toward money. A new practice called financial therapy is bridging the gap between those two worlds."

My interest in this field led me to the Financial Recovery Institute, which was started by Karen McCall in the USA in 1988. I experienced the benefits of money coaching under Karen and became a licensed

Financial Recovery Coach. Using the unique processes and money management tools developed by the Institute, I can help you:

- Gain clarity about your personal and business finances and stop living from paycheck to paycheck;
- Understand why you fall into debt and develop a plan to stay out of debt;
- Prioritise your spending so that you spend in a way that feels good to you, aligned with your true values, goals and desires;
- Initiate fruitful money conversations with your loved ones without fear or guilt;
- Pick yourself up financially and emotionally after job loss or divorce;
- Create a money fitness plan so that you will feel confident and secure about the future;
- Improve your earning capacity and the reason why you are "under-earning."

FINALLY ...

I hope more women will come forward to share their stories and confront their money demons. There is a general impression that Singapore is a very materialistic society and in order to live well and be respected on this small island, one has to be a millionaire – or at least behave like one.

However, through my journey of writing this book, I realised that there are indeed many roads to financial freedom. We have the power to shape our lives and our financial futures in a way that is meaningful to us, without any apology or shame.

WHERE TO FIND HELP AND INFORMATION

For every money and emotional struggle we face, there's help and support. Here's a listing of educational resources, counselling organisations, women's groups, blogs and websites that I recommend. This is not an exhaustive list and some of the listings may only apply to readers living in my home country Singapore. However, I hope that this modest listing will prompt readers to embark on their own research to empower themselves with knowledge and insights in their journey to attain financial independence.

Financial Education

The following websites provide free online education, events and seminars on financial planning and investment fundamentals:

MoneySense http://www.moneysense.gov.sg
This is a national financial education programme for Singapore, providing essential information to help you understand financial planning.

Securities Investors Association (Singapore) SIAS http://www. sias.org.sg

A non-profit membership organisation focusing on investor education and representation. Membership at SGD$12 a year, gives you online access to its training videos and podcasts.

CPF Singapore https://www.cpf.gov.sg The Central Provident Fund (CPF) is a comprehensive social security system that enables working Singapore citizens and permanent residents to set aside funds for retirement, as well as healthcare, home ownership, family protection and asset enhancement. Check out the handy retirement calculator to calculate your retirement income.

Investopedia   http://www.investopedia.com/university/ beginner The world's largest financial education website, Investopedia offers timely, trusted and actionable financial information for every investor. They even offer a free online tutorial on investment.

Other Web Resources

www.wisebread.com This website is a guide on how to live well and spend wisely – packed with advice and ideas on money making and money saving.

www.peakprosperity/crashcourse This is an animated, easy-to-understand video course on the global monetary system and economy, created by Chris Martenson – an independent US analyst and blogger who goes behind the headlines.

www.moneysmart.sg A go-to guide for researching the best home and car loans, credit cards and insurance solutions in Singapore, as well as blogs on personal finance and investment.

Counselling

These organisations provide counselling on legal, marital and financial matters in Singapore. Similar services exist in most countries and communities. Check the internet to find the one closest to you.

AWARE (Association of Women for Action and Research) www. aware.org.sg/legal-clinic
AWARE offers a free legal clinic twice a month with experienced lawyers to provide women with legal information and advice. Its team of volunteer lawyers will explain your legal rights and options in a wide range of areas during a single 30 minute consultation. Call its Helpline (1800 774 5935) to make an appointment.

Credit Counselling Singapore www.ccs.org.sg A registered charity and non-profit organisation, CCS helps people with unsecured consumer debt problems through education and debt repayment plans.

EMCC www.emcc.org.sg EMCC provides marriage retreats, mediation and counselling. Its team of highly qualified counsellors help couples to discuss topics like child rearing, finances, life goals and to work out any issues.

Focus on the Family www.family.org.sg A worldwide Christian organisation that promotes family harmony, Focus on the Family organises regular workshops and courses for couples to improve their communication, manage each other's expectations and strengthen their relationship.

National Council on Problem Gambling www.ncpg.org.sg Comprising 17 council members with expertise in psychiatry and psychology, social services, counselling, legal, rehabilitative as well as religious services, NCPG provides a web counselling service and helpline for problem gamblers and their family members in Singapore. To curb gambling addiction, NCPG can also issue casiono exclusions and visit limits.

Entrepreneur and Women's Support Groups

Betty Ashman www.bettyashman.com Founded by Betty Ashman, an entrepreneur, consultant, author and mum, this website connects you to a community of women entrepreneurs and business owners who provide products, ideas and events to help you get started with a business of your own.

IWFCI Singapore (International Women's Federation for Commerce and Industry) www.iwfcis.org.sg IWFCI is a global business network that promotes international trade opportunities among its 2 million affiliated members worldwide. It has chapters in Australia, Malaysia, Singapore and India.

Lean In www.leanincircles.org A follow up from Sheryl Sandberg's book Lean In, LeanIn.org is committed to offering women the ongoing inspiration and support to help them achieve their goals. LeanIn encourages women to create their own special interest group and networks via LeanIn circles. There are 27,000 LeanIn circles in 141 countries worldwide. You can start a LeanIn circle or join an existing one related to your area of interest.

Mums@Work Singapore www.mumsatwork.net Founded in early 2010 by Sher-li, a 'mumpreneur', this is the first career portal in Singapore that supports women to find the perfect balance between being a mum and working. It is a go-to source for mothers seeking flexi-work arrangements, job openings and business opportunities as 'mumpreneurs'.

The Athena Network Singapore www.theathenanetwork.com.sg A diverse and dynamic business networking group of working women and entrepreneurs, Athena organises monthly coffee morning, networking luncheons and social evenings to share knowledge and expertise.

Woolfworks www.woolfworks.sg Provides a shared workspace and community for women in central Singapore. Woolfworks' members are freelancers, business owners, writers, remote corporate workers, flexi-workers, coaches, consultants and 'thinking-about-it-preneurs.'

Printed in the United States
By Bookmasters